Enveloped in Light
The Tallit Sourcebook

Books by Dov Peretz Elkins

The Bible's Top Fifty Ideas: The Essential Concepts Everyone Should Know
(with Abigail Treu)

Enveloped in Light: The Tallit Sourcebook
(with Steven Schwarzman)

Moments of the Spirit: Quotations That Inspire, Inform and Involve

Chicken Soup for the Jewish Soul (coauthor)

A Treasury of Israel & Zionism: A Sourcebook for Writers,
Speakers and Educators

A Shabbat Reader

Moments of Transcendence

Jewish Guided Imagery

Forty Days of Transformation

Meditations for the Days of Awe

Shepherd of Jerusalem

God's Warriors: Rabbis in Uniform

So Young To Be a Rabbi

A Tradition Reborn

Prescription for a Long and Happy Life

My Seventy-Two Friends: Encounters with Refuseniks in the USSR

God's Warriors: Dramatic Adventures of Rabbis in Uniform

Four Questions on the Sidrah

Sidrah Sparks

More Sidrah Sparks

Clarifying Jewish Values

Jewish Consciousness Raising

Loving My Jewishness

Experiential Programs for Jewish Groups

Teaching People to Love Themselves

Glad To Be Me: Building Self-Esteem in Yourself and Others

Twelve Pathways to Feeling Better About Yourself

Self Concept Sourcebook

Translations
Melodies From My Father's House – by Simcha Raz
Hasidic Wisdom (translated with Jonathan Elkins) – by Simcha Raz

Children's Book
Seven Delightful Stories for Every Day

Enveloped in Light
The Tallit Sourcebook

Edited by
Dov Peretz Elkins and Steven Schwarzman

POMEGRANATE BOOKS
An Imprint of Growth Associates Publishers
Princeton, New Jersey

ISBN 0-918834-26-0
Library of Congress Control Number: 2004114926

Printed in Israel.
All rights reserved.

This book was designed by Susan Klingman
and set in Palatino Linotype.

For a complete catalog of books contact:

Pomegranate Books
Growth Associates Publishers
212 Stuart Road East
Princeton, NJ 08540-1946
609-497-7375
Fax: 609-497-0325
E-mail: Office@JewishGrowth.org
www.JewishGrowth.org

Contents

Introduction

Introduction
Steven Schwarzman

As far as we can tell, this book is the first attempt to bring together a wide variety of sources available in English on the subject of the tallit. In the pages that follow, you can find contributions by a Nobel Prize winner along with everyday people, rabbis and professors along with poets and Internet journalists. By design, we've included such different voices in hopes of producing a composite picture; just as the tallit is a very democratic garment, making the audacious statement that each one of us has within us the mark of royalty ~ while at the same time, enveloping us in a coziness that marks our relationship with God.

If the only טַלִיתוֹת (*tallitot*) you've worn are the child-sized ones on the rack at your synagogue, you've been missing out. (Whoever invented those deserves some kind of anti-prize for a significant contribution to the despiritualization of the prayer experience.) Jews pray as a community, but before this communal prayer can begin, the individuals wrap themselves in their tallitot for a moment, shutting out the rest of the world for a quiet second or two in order to get ready to join it. Children can hide themselves in a parent's tallit, and indeed there is a custom during the Priestly Blessing to cover one's children in the tallit. When you wear a full-sized tallit, you will never be at a loss over what to do with your hands. One side is always in need of a little tug to adjust it, or a big one to bring it back up onto your shoulder when it falls. Fix one side, and the other will probably need a fix as a result. And the צִיצָת (*tzitzit*), in addition to their ritual purposes, are always good for keeping a small child occupied while on a parent's lap.

My own tallit is now precisely 20 years old, a wedding present from my wife, Bettina. Until we went shopping for it in Jerusalem, I had never noticed the subtle differences between one tallit and another ~ and that was just in the traditional black stripes model. Now the white is yellowed a bit, a fact I mark with pride, as it indicates how long this tallit has been with me, I with it, and of course, my wife and I with each other. It's not the only Jewish symbol in our home ~ far from it ~ but my tallit is the one I treasure most. It is mine in a most personal way.

The tallit has been around for a few thousand years (as you will learn in some of the historically-oriented contributions herein), but there have also been some exciting developments in just the last few decades as the recipe for תְּכֵלֶת (*tekhelet*) ~ the blue dye for tzitzit ~ has apparently been rediscovered and women have begun (or begun again, as you will read!) to wear tallitot in some communities. We hope that this sourcebook will help more people learn about the beauty of the tallit and its rich potential as a ritual item in adding a spiritual and ethical dimension to Jewish prayer and life.

The Tallit and its Messages

The Tallit and Its Messages
Dov Peretz Elkins

When the intellectual giant of East European Jewry, the Vilna Gaon, was on his deathbed, he wept bitterly. Asked to explain, he replied that his sadness came from knowing that he would soon leave such a wonderful world in which it is possible to fulfill the divine behest of wearing tzitzit for just a few *groschen*. The Vilna Gaon was not the only Jew in history who experienced such ecstasy by wearing the Biblically-commanded prayer shawl. Jews from Talmudic days to contemporary times have considered wearing the tallit one of the great privileges of being a partner in the Covenant of Abraham.

Close your eyes and picture a synagogue in which Jews are gathered for prayer. The impressionistic scene which the mind's eye reveals is a sea of white, men covered with the tallit draped on their backs and shoulders, swaying back and forth in the mystic rhythm of ancient Hebrew liturgy. A Jew would feel almost naked singing the morning prayers without a tallit.

Given the traditional reverence for this ancient garment of worship, what meaning has it for the contemporary Jew? Is its usage merely blind acceptance of the chain of tradition? Or can contemporary man wrest from the ancient lines of the Biblical text, and from the subsequent writings of pious students throughout the ages, some sense of purpose to ennoble our own lives, to enrich our own existence?

In his essay on "The Music of Poetry," T. S. Eliot propounds a startling thesis about poetry that applies with equal force to ritual (which, after all, is poetry made visual). "A poem may appear to mean very different things to different readers, and all of these meanings may be different from what the author thought he meant." Notice particularly the phrase, "what the author *thought* he meant." Does not an author *know* what he means? "The reader's interpretation," continues Eliot, "may differ from the author's and be equally valid ~ it may even be better." Further: "There may be much more in a poem than the author was aware of."[1]

For our purposes, what this means is that rituals, like poems, are creations, in a way similar to persons. Our parents plant the seeds that bring us here and launch us into the world, but once arrived we are on our own. We live a separate existence from our parent-creators.

So, too, with a ritual or a poem. The creator might have had one idea in mind, but the creature is free to be explained and interpreted in a myriad of ways. Surely the Biblical writer knew why the tassels were to be worn. But the tasseled *tallit* is a creature that has existed, in various forms, some three thousand years, and has all along accumulated many new faces and shades of coloration in purpose and meaning.

Some of these meanings still speak to contemporary man. Surely no one person at any given time will feel all the beauty and joy and mystery felt by all the interpreters of the tallit throughout history. Different meanings will relate differently to different worshippers. Our purpose in this essay will be to review a number of the most meaningful messages that the *tallit* with its four tassels has suggested to sensitive souls throughout history.

For purposes of clarity we shall divide these layers of meaning into five primary categories: symbolic, esthetic, historical-national, ideological-ethical, and metaphysical.

Symbolic

The oldest, and therefore the classical, interpretation of the tassels (a better translation of *tzitzit* than fringes ~ the latter are projecting threads on the edge of a fabric, not a knotted cluster on the corner[2]) is found in Numbers 15:37-41:

> *Adonai spoke to Moses, saying: Speak to the Israelite people and instruct them to make tassels on the corners of their garments forever. Let them attach a cord of blue to the tassel on each corner. That shall be called tzitzit. Look at it and recall all Adonai's commandments (mitzvot) and perform them, so that you will not lustfully follow your heart and eyes. Thus shall you be reminded to keep all My commandments and to be holy to your God. I am Adonai your God, Who brought you out of the land of Egypt to be your God. I am Adonai your God!*

The tassel, the צִיצָת (*tzitzit*), therefore, is to remind its wearer to lead a holy life. Originally, the tzitzit was worn on one's daily garments. Later, when clothing styles changed from the four-cornered toga to fitted garments, a four-cornered shawl or tallit (probably from the same Greek word that produced the English word *stole*) was donned only during hours of prayer. Very observant Jews, trying to stay as close as possible to the original intent of the Torah, wear a four-cornered undergarment all day, called a טַלִּית קָטָן (*tallit katan*), or small tallit.

Thus, when worn on one's daily outer garment, the tzitzit easily pointed to its referent, the mitzvot, and their ultimate goal: to lead a Jew to a life of holiness. R. Brasch has written:

The tallit is the badge of the army of God's servants,
where the only distinction is that of holiness. It is a
vestment engendering a feeling of dedication to a life
in the service of God. It speaks, too, of the universality
of God and the unity of man. It is a perpetual reminder
that no pattern of living can be of lasting value unless
it is cut from the cloth of religion.[3]

The צִיצָת (*tzitzit*), then, is a symbol. Through a three-staged process ~ looking, remembering, performing[4] ~ the צִיצָת (*tzitzit*) reminds its wearer of the six hundred and thirteen mitzvot enjoined in Rabbinic tradition.[5] Performing the mitzvot, in turn, leads one to a life of holiness: dedication, commitment, uniqueness, moral and spiritual purity.

This sublime cause would be sufficient to give the tallit and its tasseled corners reason to exist. Like a flag whose colors, shape and design conjure up the country which it stands for, with all its high ideals, historical struggles, and inspiration to patriotism, so the tasseled vestment represents the life of the Jew, with its thrust towards morality, its repeated battles for redemption, and its chosen position for service to God among the peoples of the world.

"Look at it (the tzitzit) and remember all My
commandments." This may be compared to a man
struggling for his life in a raging sea. The captain of
the ship threw him a rope, saying: 'Take hold of it or
perish.' Similarly, God says to Israel, 'As long as
you cling to the tzitzit, you will not perish' (Bemidbar
Rabbah 17:7).

The tallit and צִיצָת (*tzitzit*) are symbolic reminders, visual stimuli. Their goal is that their wearer will be goaded to performing the mitzvot and fulfilling their purpose of seeking a life of holiness.

Esthetic

While the primary importance of wearing a tasseled shawl during worship is to remind one of the mitzvot and their underlying purpose of leading a holy life, there are countless other nuances that help account for the millennia-old popularity of the tallit. We alluded to this in referring earlier to T. S. Eliot's statement that interpretations of poetry (ritual) can be multiplied according to the tastes and insights of the reader (practitioner).

The physical beauty of the tallit has contributed significantly to its universal acceptance. It is often made of wool or silk; sometimes blanketing the entire back of the worshipper and sometimes draped neatly around the neck; sometimes with black or blue stripes, and often with none; on occasion it will be cream-colored, at other times pure white. Regardless of size, color, decorations, and other differentiating stylistic qualities, the tallit has been a popular object of the artistic talents of weavers, designers and craftspersons through the ages. It is fashionable among many observant Jews to acquire one tallit for daily prayers and another for Shabbat and festivals ~ the latter garment being even more elaborate and esthetically appealing. It is a sign of piety to take a measure of pride in selecting a tallit that is pleasing to the eye as well as to the heart.

There is halakhic precedent for this. It is not entirely a matter of materialistic satisfaction in looking attractive in private prayer or in the synagogue. An ancient value concept[6] of Jewish theology is that of הִדּוּר מִצְוָה *(hiddur mitzvah),* or adornment of a commandment.[7] To be truly pious, it is not sufficient merely to carry out the letter of the law. It should be done in a way that brings a sense of beauty and grace to the performance of the mitzvah. For the carrying out of a religious precept, one should be generous with his means and his effort, and not do it in a perfunctory way.

In the Song of the Sea, in which Moses praises God for delivering the Israelites from their Egyptian pursuers, we find the verse: "This is my God and I will glorify Adonai, the God of my fathers and I will exalt the One" (Exodus 15:2). The Midrash elucidates this verse in the following words: "Is it possible for a creature of flesh and blood to add glory to his Creator? It means this: I will be beautiful before God in carrying out the mitzvot. I will make God a lovely לוּלָב *(lulav),* a beautiful סֻכָּה *(sukkah),* attractive צִיצָת *(tzitzit),* handsome tefillin."[8]

This love and appreciation of art and physical beauty in the service of God is in complete consonance with Judaism's view of man and the universe and the absence within it of the dichotomy found in other traditions between mind and body, spirit and letter, the spiritual and the physical.[9]

Thus, in American Judaism, it is not uncommon to find synagogues created by leading architects, sanctuaries appointed with highly attractive furnishings as well as holy objects, and a genuine attempt to make the experience of worship esthetically appealing as well as religiously inspiring. The purchase and use, and sometimes the personal creation, of an attractive and appealing tallit is a natural outgrowth of this philosophy of positive emphasis on physical beauty.

Historical-National

The close association of the tallit and its symbolism with the history and national pride of the Jewish people is a prominent example of the difficulty of drawing a sharp distinction between the religious and the secular in Jewish tradition.

Tracing its origins as far back as the days of Moses, the tallit creates a bond uniting Jewry today with its Biblical ancestors, as well as with all the intervening generations.

The "Founding Fathers" of political Zionism thought it entirely appropriate to select the colors of the Jewish garment of religious worship for the creation of the flag-emblem of the new movement of Jewish national renaissance. Now universally recognized as the flag of the sovereign State of Israel, the blue stripes on white background, with the blue Star of David emblazoned upon it, are a modern reincarnation of the charge found in Numbers 15:37-41.

We are indeed fortunate to have preserved for us a detailed record of the thoughts in the mind of the Zionist leader who designed the Jewish national flag, later destined to become the Israeli flag. The blue-and-white flag was first unfurled at the First Zionist Congress in Basle, in 1897. David Wolffsohn, a British Jew who was to succeed Theodor Herzl in 1905 as President of the World Zionist Organization, left this account of how he came to design the flag:

> *At the behest of our leader, Herzl, I came to Basle to make preparations for the Zionist Congress, to assure its success and to avoid any opening for detractors. Among the many problems that occupied me then was one which contained something of the essence of the Jewish problem. What flag would we hang in the Congress Hall? . . . Then an idea struck me. We have a flag ~ and it is blue and white. The talith with which we wrap ourselves when we pray: that is our symbol. Let us take this talith from its bag and unroll it before the eyes of Israel and the eyes of all nations. So I ordered a blue and white flag with the Shield of David painted upon it. That is how our national flag, that flew over Congress Hall, came into being. And no one expressed any surprise or asked whence it came or how.*

It is fitting at this point to explain further the colors of blue and white and their origin and significance. In the Biblical command, each tassel is to have a cord of blue (Numbers 15:38). The Talmud[10] comments on this Scriptural passage: "Why blue? Because blue resembles the sea, and the sea resembles the heavens, and the heavens resemble the Throne of Glory, as it is said: 'And there was under God's feet a paved work of [blue] sapphire stone, like the very heaven in purity' (Exodus 24:10) and 'the likeness of a throne, as the appearance of a sapphire stone'" (Ezekiel 1:26).

The blue against the white brings to mind visions of the jeweled colors of the sea, the heavens, and God's Throne of Glory, in their pristine purity and sanctity. Fitting colors to choose for the symbolic transposition of a people's ideals and aspirations into a cloth representation!

The modern flag of Israel, the people and the State, thus combines in one emblem the religious meaning of the eternal covenant between God and Israel, and the corporate solidarity of God's eternal people.

At this point, the reader may well ask: Why is there no cord of blue in many tallitot (plural of tallit) today? The blue coloration was taken from a shellfish known as a mollusk (*hilazon*) which was found on the Mediterranean shores and which subsequently became extinct. Rather than use an imitation, the

Rabbis preferred to eliminate the use of blue completely.

There is great irony in the fact that a religious precept was to become the source of the symbol of a modern secular, political movement, and ultimately of a national state. Many of the founders of modern Zionism and Israel were imbued with secular socialist ideals. Along with emigration from the ghettos and towns of Eastern Europe to the Land of the Dream, came the rejection of outward religious forms, such as prayer and ritual. The Jewish renaissance was to be built on lofty principles of socialist philosophy and Biblical ethics. But the "narrow particularism" of concrete symbols, such as the wearing of tallit and tefillin, was to have no part in the rebuilding of the Jewish homeland. Its character was to be more universal and more ideological than medieval Judaism would sanction.

Joseph Baratz, for example, founded the first collective farm settlement in the Middle East, Kibbutz Degania, in 1909. Like many in his generation, Baratz gave away the tallit he had brought with him from Russia at age 18. However, advancing years have a way of bringing one back to one's early training, and Baratz was to change his mind. His daughter, Yona Baratz Shapiro, still living in Degania, told an American reporter recently: "When my father was over 80, he wrote a note that we found only after he died. He asked to be buried in his prayer shawl, because that is the custom among observant Jews."[11]

A fascinating tale about a tallit emerged from the 1973 Yom Kippur War. It first appeared in *BaMahane*, weekly of the Israel Defense Forces, and was later retold in the *Jerusalem Post Weekly* of November 13, 1973. It is a story told by Eyal, a twenty-year-old tank commander from Ramat HaSharon. On the second day of the war, Eyal's tank was hit while trying to stem the Egyptian attack across the Suez Canal. With a group of forty-two other soldiers, he hid in the Sinai desert marshes, not far from the Canal. At daybreak, they were spotted, but managed to escape under fire to an abandoned house in Kantara. Being detected again, they crawled back to the marshes and remained there overnight, only a short distance from Egyptian tanks and artillery batteries. "By daybreak," explained Eyal, "we were in the middle of the marshes. We ... heard tanks approaching. They were our tanks. But how could we identify ourselves before they opened fire on us? One of the boys, a *yeshiva bocher*, had an idea. He took out his tallit and ran towards the tanks, waving it. The tanks did not open fire. Our men recognized the tallit: it saved us from certain death."

It is the custom among Jewish worshippers to gather the four tassels *(tzitziyot)* of the tallit and wrap them around the finger just before reciting the morning Sh'ma, as the following words are recited:

Bring us safely from the four corners of the earth,
And lead us in dignity to our Holy Land.
You, O God, are the Source of deliverance;
You have chosen us from all peoples and tongues.

It is most fitting, therefore, for the tallit ~ whose four corners have been gathered together daily for centuries, signifying the dignified restoration of a Jewish national homeland in the Land of our Fathers ~ to be utilized in the newly-created State of Israel as its national emblem and, as instanced in the story of Eyal, as a coat of arms to identify a struggling brother who is in need of the deliverance and salvation of another Jew.

Ideological-Ethical

There are at least six reasons for wearing the tallit, offered by various writers, that fall under the rubric of ideological-ethical considerations.

Democracy

The wearing of a prayer shawl by all adult worshippers[12] can be seen as an example of the democratization of Judaism in post-Biblical times. With the destruction of the Temple in Jerusalem, official Jewish public worship was authorized wherever ten Jews gathered, anywhere in the world, with or without benefit of clergy. In other religious traditions, it is often the case that only the *leader* of worship is permitted to wear cultic vestments. In Judaism, the striving for holiness devolves upon everyone, not only the "clergy." Thus, the fulfillment of the mitzvot, and the wearing of the tzitzit to remind one of this obligation, are the right and duty of every Jew.

Freedom

In the Passover Haggadah, the Scriptural paragraph that commands the Israelites to wear צִיצַת (*tzitzit*) on the corners of their garments (Numbers 15:37-41) is referred to as *Yetziat Mitzrayim* - the Going Out of Egypt. Rabbi Eleazar ben Azariah discusses the question of whether a Jew is obligated to recite this paragraph, the third paragraph of the Sh'ma, only in the morning, or at night also.[13] To him, its significance lay in the last verse of the section: "I am Adonai your God Who brought you out of the land of Egypt to be your God." To Rabbi Eleazar it is God's role as Redeemer of mankind that is prominent, and it is this role that he would emphasize in heeding the command to wear צִיצַת (*tzitzit*).

Others point out that in ancient times slaves wore short robes in order to move about quickly and easily and do the bidding of their masters. Free men, on the other hand, wore long flowing togas decorated with fringes. When a Jew stood before God in prayer, he was to do so as a free person. In like manner, during the Passover Seder, it is the custom to recline in symbolic remembrance of the behavior of free men in antiquity.[14]

Rabbi Mordecai M. Kaplan, revered master and scholar of American Judaism, has offered yet another reason why the tallit symbolizes the freedom of the Jew. According to Rabbi Kaplan, the reason we no longer use the cord of blue in the tassel of the tallit is not because the dye from the mollusk is no longer available. The real explanation, according to this theory, is that the color blue was the sign of the Roman Emperor, and anyone not of royalty who dared to wear it would be executed. Wearing such a cord of blue on one's religious garment would signify rejection of the supreme authority of the Emperor. By specifically wearing the cord of blue on the tallit, the Jew was proclaiming his faith in the Kingship of God and was declaring his faith in God's commandments and laws; this helped him avoid giving in to his passions and yielding to his temptations of aggression and lust. According to Rabbi Kaplan, the function of the tallit is to draw attention to the purpose and meaning of the laws of the Torah.[15] True freedom means obeying God's laws, and not worshipping flesh and blood ~ an emperor, king, or human leader.

Peace

Another fascinating and imaginative explanation for the blue cord in the tassel on the tallit is offered by the late Hebrew poet laureate of Palestine, Hayim Nahman Bialik (d. 1934). In his essays, *Devarim Shebe-al Peh*, Bialik suggested that mixing a thread of blue linen among the other fringes, which were made of wool, was a unique departure from the ordinary prohibition of mixing wool and linen in the same garment (Deuteronomy 22:11-12). According to this view, the Biblical prohibition grew out of a history of quarreling between shepherds, who wore woolen garments, and farmers, who wore linen apparel. A person who wore such a mixture of linen and wool would expose himself to danger, because a member of his tribe might mistake him for one of the other side and attack him. Combining both wool (the fringes) and linen (the blue cord) in one garment became an act of reconciliation, making the tallit a symbol of peace and harmony.[16]

Humility

One of the Hasidic masters, Rabbi Yehezkel of Kozmer, was once asked why it is that the blessing pronounced upon donning the tallit contains the words לְהִתְעַטֵף בַּצִיצָת (*lehitatef batzitzit*) ~ to wrap oneself in the צִיצָת (*tzitzit*) ~ but nowhere mentions the word טַלִית (*tallit*). Yet, in actuality we wrap ourselves in the טַלִית (*tallit*), not in the צִיצָת (*tzitzit*). The צִיצָת (*tzitzit*) trail almost to the ground, he explained, and thus the law requires that we say the blessing over them as a reminder of the need to be humble. Whoever is humble is in truth lofty; and whoever is haughty, is in truth lowly.[17]

Repentance

Another Hasidic teacher contrasts the appearance of a person before an earthly ruler, pleading before him in black mourning clothes, with the people of Israel who plead for forgiveness before God arrayed in white (the tallit), knowing that all who return with a full heart to their Maker will receive pardon at God's hands.[18]

Against Hypocrisy

Rabbi Norman Lamm, in an essay called "On Showing Your True Colors,"[19] points out that the absence of the blue thread in the צִיצָת (*tzitzit*) today is a solemn warning against hypocrisy and deception. Quoting the Talmudic Rabbis, who say in God's name: "I will punish one who affixes a thread of blue dyed with indigo and pretends that it is really blue from a mollusk" (Bava Metzia 61b), Lamm makes an excellent case for the modern-day tallit without blue as a symbol of sincerity and authenticity. Too many of us would be willing to pass off indigo, a common and inexpensive vegetable dye, for the real blue of the extinct shellfish. The Talmud demands that we show our true colors in all matters, ethical as well as ritual. We must be honest to ourselves and honest to our fellow humans. The absence of blue in the טַלִּית (*tallit*) is a wholesome reminder of this lesson in ethical living.

Metaphysical

Perhaps the peak of religious exhilaration that is reached through wearing the tallit is the spiritual ecstasy that one achieves both in the process of covering oneself with it and in wearing it.

While all the intellectual reasons for wearing such a religious vestment appeal to the mind of a worshipping Jew, it is the feeling, which cannot be put in words, that is probably most important in making the tallit a key to depth in the prayer experience. It is the feeling of being infused with the spirit of the Divine Presence ~ שְׁכִינָה (*Shekhinah*) that the tallit provides for the worshipper. While many modern Jews wear their tallit folded and draped around the neck like a scarf, many more traditional observers literally cover their entire body from neck to heels with the long, woolen tallit. Furthermore, when first putting it on, the custom is to wrap it totally around the head so that one becomes lost in deep thought and prayer, in intensive religious feeling, as one seeks to enter the mood for fervent prayer.

A generation ago, use of such a large tallit and the custom of burying one's head in deep meditation and prayer while the tallit covers the face, would have been thought to smack of "old-time" Judaism. Yet today one finds many young as well as mature people deriving authentic meaning out of the traditional usage of the large wool tallit. Perhaps it is the influence of the customs of *Eretz Yisrael,* or the various cults of meditation, or the popularity of Eastern mystical philosophies that have reawakened interest in these emotional aspects of traditional Jewish prayer.

Whether one uses the large or small tallit, and whether one prefers to cover his head in the tallit while reciting the introductory blessing or not, Jewish tradition long ago recognized the mystical value of a prayer shawl in readying the mind and heart for prayer. One cannot cease one activity and immediately turn to an intensive religious experience such as prayer without some transitional aids to bridge the gap. The tallit serves this function well, as the ancient Rabbis saw with great clarity and insight.

An ancient rabbi taught:

> *When the children of Israel are wrapped in their tallit, let them feel as though the glory of the Divine Presence were upon them. For Scripture does not say: 'That you may look upon it [the tzitzit],' but rather 'That you may look upon God (Numbers 15:39),' that is, upon the Holy One, blessed is God.*[20]

The tallit has been compared to the sheltering wings of the Divine Presence in that the Hebrew word for wing, כָּנָף (*kanaf*) is the same word for "corner" that is used in the Biblical paragraph commanding use of the tzitzit. The essence of the tallit, of course, is in the corner (כָּנָף - *kanaf*) where the tassel hangs. Likewise, the essence of the feeling one derives from wearing the tallit is the feeling of being covered by the wings of the Divine Presence.

Various suggestions have been made for meditations prior to donning the tallit, which help create the mood of reverence and sanctity, of being sheltered under the wings of the שְׁכִינָה (*Shekhinah*). One is from Psalms 104:1-2:

> *Bless Adonai, O my soul! O Lord, my God, You are very great; You are clothed in glory and majesty, wrapped in a robe of light; You spread out the heavens like a tent cloth.*

A second suggested meditation comes from the medieval works of the Kabbalists, mystics who contributed much to the later movement of mystical thought and practice known as Hasidism. Such a Kabbalistic meditation is called a כַּוָּנָה (*kavanah*) ~ literally, "intention"; a prayer focusing one's intention preparatory to the performing of a mitzvah. One kavanah reads:

> *I am here enwrapping myself in this fringed robe, in fulfillment of the command of my Creator, as it is written in the Torah: 'They shall make them a fringe upon the corners of their garments throughout their generations.' And even as I cover myself with the Tallith in this world, so may my soul deserve to be clothed with a beauteous spiritual robe in the world to come, in the garden of Eden. Amen.*[21]

These, then, are some of the meanings and interpretations ~ symbolic, esthetic, historical-national, ideological-ethical, and metaphysical ~ that have been found in this simple yet lovely prayer shawl, the tallit. It has been a revered garment for millennia, and most certainly will remain so in the future.

Before we conclude this brief overview of some of the meanings of the tallit, it would be well to relate two brief incidents that buttress the thesis of the centuries-long indispensability of the tallit to the Jew.

One tale comes from fifteenth-century Sicily. In 1493, the Jews of that island were stripped of all their possessions and sent from their homes. Before departing, they made one simple request, though it was ultimately denied: that in quitting Sicily they be privileged to take with them one thing: their tallitot.[22]

The final tale emerged from the prison walls of Soviet Russia in 1969. Patricia Blake, correspondent of the now-defunct *The Reporter* magazine, visited Moscow, and upon the advice of an American rabbi brought with her some tallitot for distribution. After letting it be known that she had a number of tallitot with her, she returned to her hotel room. After a short while, an elderly Jew knocked at the door. He asked her for a tallit. She then pointed to a ventilator in the ceiling, suggesting that a microphone was concealed there and that caution should be employed in conversation. But instead of whispering to her, he cried out: "Are you telling me this place is full of spies? Don't you suppose I know all about it? What can they do to me? I'm 74 years old. I'm retired; I have no job to be fired from. My whole family was killed by the Germans. But you see, with a *tallis*, I can die!"[23]

For this aged suffering Jew, a tallit made death tolerable. For others, a tallit may make life more meaningful and enriching. Perhaps a deeper understanding of some of its meanings and its history will help make it so.

---

[1] On *Poetry and Poets* (New York: Noonday Press, paperback edition, 1961), p. 23.

[2] Cf. David Kline, "Instead of Tying Yourself in Knots," *Sh'ma*, January 25, 1974, p. 46.

[3] *The Judaic Heritage: Its Teachings, Philosophy, and Symbols* (New York: David McKay Co., Inc., 1969), p. 243.

[4] Cf. Menahot 43b: "Seeing alerts the memory and memory leads to action."

[5] In Talmudic numerology, the value of the Hebrew letters in the word *tzitzit* is 600. Together with the 8 strings and 5 knots of each tassel, the total is 613.

[6] For a fuller interpretation of the meaning of "value concepts" in Judaism, see the works of Max Kadushin, especially *Worship and Ethics: A Study in Rabbinic Judaism* (Evanston: Northwestern University Press, 1964), pp. 20-26.

[7] Cf. Bava Kamma 9b.

[8] *Mekhilta* on Exodus 15:2 (Horowitz and Rabin edition, p. 127 and parallels listed there).

[9] Cf. Milton Steinberg, *Basic Judaism* (New York: Harcourt Brace and Co., 1947), pp. 71-75.

[10] Menahot 43b.

[11] *The Boston Globe,* August 20, 1973, p. 11.

[12] Usually only males wear the tallit, but today some females are beginning to experiment with using it. There is no halakhic reason why they should not, even though according to traditional law only adult males are *obligated* to wear one.

[13] Cf. Mishnah Berakhot 1:5.

[14] Cf. Roland B. Gittelsohn, *The Meaning of Judaism* (New York: World Publishing Co., 1970), pp. 135-136.

[15] *Proceedings of the Rabbinical Assembly, Vol. 33* (New York: The Rabbinical Assembly, 1969), p. 35.

[16] Cf. Solomon D. Goldfarb, *Lev VeLashon* (New York: printed privately, 1968), pp. 112-113.

[17] Mordechai HaKohen, *Al HaTorah* (Jerusalem: Reuven Mass, 1968), cf. on Deuteronomy 22:12 (*gedilim*), p. 547.

[18] Quoted by R. Brasch, *op. cit.,* p. 239.

[19] In *The Royal Reach: Discourses on the Jewish Tradition and the World Today* (New York: Phillip Feldheim, Inc., 1970), pp. 246-251.

[20] *Midrash Tehillim* 90:18.

---

[21] Joseph H. Hertz, *The Authorised Daily Prayer Book* (New York: Bloch Publishing Co., 1957), p. 45.

[22] Abraham E. Millgram, *Jewish Worship* (Philadelphia: The Jewish Publication Society of America, 1971), p. 345.

[23] Quoted in Samuel Chiel, *Spectators or Participants* (New York: Jonathan David Publishers, 1969), pp. 159-160.

The Tallit in Sermons
and Commentaries

A Message from Outer Space
Jack Riemer

Part of my message is going to be really far out. (I
know that there are some readers who think that this
is true of many of my messages, but this time it is
really so.) My message is in three parts: the first part
comes from the Bible, the second from Philadelphia,
and the third from outer space.

Let me begin with the words from the Bible:

> *And Adonai spoke unto Moses, saying "speak unto
> the Israelites and bid them make fringes in the corners
> of their garments throughout their generations....that
> you may remember to do all My commandments and
> to be holy to your God."* (Numbers 15:37-41)

Do you recognize these words? They are the last
paragraph of the Sh'ma. And they are the origin of the
tallit, which is the Jewish prayer costume.

The tallit is a very important Jewish educational instrument. It binds us to our past. It connects us with the going out of Egypt. It binds us to our God. It is a public thing that we share with other Jews. And it is an intimate private thing, because when we wrap ourselves in the tallit, for one precious moment, body and soul, we are alone with our God. And when we look upon it, we are reminded of all the rest of the commandments of Adonai that we may do them.

That the tallit is a precious part of the Jewish tradition ~ this is the first part of my message.

The second part of my message is this: It has never been the feeling of Jews that it is enough simply to do a mitzvah. If you are going to do it, Jews have always felt, you ought to do it with beauty and with enthusiasm and with a sense of aesthetics. And so down through the centuries Jews have practiced what we call הִדּוּר מִצְוָה (*hiddur mitzvah*), which means doing a mitzvah with beauty and with grace.

So, for example, technically you could just put up a shack and it would be a kosher sukkah, but there is no Jew in the world who would do that. If you are going to have a sukkah, then you adorn it and you decorate it and you make it a thing of beauty. And so it is with a Sefer Torah or a mezuzah or an Aron Kodesh, and so it is with every other Jewish ritual object. We not only have them, we decorate them and we design them and we adorn them and we try to make them things of beauty, works of art.

And so it is with the tallit. Technically, a person can walk into a synagogue and borrow one from the rack and fulfill his obligation. But many Jews, down through the centuries and in our own time, have felt that that was not enough. And so Jews developed the custom of weaving tallitot for themselves that would be works of art. It became a custom for this to be the gift that a bride would make or commission for her groom. Sometimes a tallit would be used as a huppah for their wedding, and then putting it on would become a daily or a weekly anniversary of how they felt on the day they were wed. And even though technically a tallit could be any color, many weavers used their imagination and made tapestries that were bold and bright and beautiful. And even though a tallit does not technically require one, it became the custom to weave a band around the edge of the tallit, called an עֲטָרָה (*atara*), in order to add to its beauty.

I have a tallit, for example, that I wear proudly, which was a gift from my wife. It has my name on one edge (so if I have an identity crisis I can look down and see who I am) and it has our wedding date on the other edge (so that I shouldn't forget to send a gift for our anniversary, God forbid, and get into trouble) and it has an atara that I think is lovely. It was made for us by Elsa Wachs of Philadelphia.

So the second part of my message is: you ought to have a tallit of your own, and not just one from the rack, and it ought to be a thing of beauty.

The third part of my message comes from outer space. Not many people seem to be aware of this, but do you know that there have been so far two Jewish astronauts? The first one was Judy Resnick of blessed memory, who died on the Challenger. The second Jewish astronaut, who for some reason seems to be less well known, is Jeffrey Hoffman. He went up into space several years ago. Jeffrey Hoffman is a member of a synagogue and a person who takes his Judaism seriously, and so he wanted his Jewishness to be a part of his journey into space with him. And so he decided to take something Jewish up into space with him.

He didn't take tefillin with him. (You know the old joke about the Jewish astronaut who keeps putting his tefillin on and off all day because the shuttle circles the globe every forty-five minutes, and every time they pass the International Date Line it is a new day and he has to daven again.) Jeffrey Hoffman didn't take his tefillin with him, but instead he took his tallit, or to be exact, he took two. He wanted his two boys who will be bar mitzvah in a few years to have a souvenir from outer space as a bar mitzvah gift. So he went to Elsa Wachs and he asked her to weave two special עֲטָרוֹת (*atarot*) for him, עֲטָרוֹת (*atarot*) that would have a space motif. (Think about that for a moment: where in the Bible does anyone go up into space? or where in the Bible is outer space mentioned?)

Elsa Wachs made the עֲטָרוֹת (atarot) for him. A few weeks later, Camp Ramah of Philadelphia had a fundraising dinner and Elsa Wachs was the guest of honor. They asked Jeffrey Hoffman to be the speaker. At the last minute he could not come because of delays in the countdown but he sent a message instead. Let me share part of that message with you:

> I was asked to come to Philadelphia to speak this evening by Mrs. Elsa Wachs. For those of you who may be unaware of our connection, let me explain that she made two magnificent עֲטָרוֹת (atarot) for me to carry into space on my flight and afterwards to present to my sons on their bar mitzvah. I wish you could see them. They are a deep purple color, hinting at the darkness of space, mixed with the blues of the earth, and with enough color tinges to suggest the spectrum that awes space travelers when they look down on earth from up above.

> The inscription on one is from Elijah and tells the story of the Chariot of Fire that took Elijah up to the heavens. The other is from the book of Job. It recalls the Voice from the whirlwind that admonished Job, "Can you cause the stars of Orion to move in their courses in the heavens? Or do you understand the Pleiades?" Are you aware of the complexity of the cosmos? I should mention that ever since I became interested in

space at around the age of six, Orion has been my favorite constellation.

My youngest son, who will receive this עֲטָרָה (*atara*), is named Orin, which is as close as my wife would let me come to my first choice for his name.

And then Jeffrey Hoffman goes on to say:

Bringing these עֲטָרוֹת (*atarot*) with me on my journey represents for me a continuity of tradition. Jews have always taken their religion and their culture with them when they moved from one country to another. I don't see why space should be any different. We are in the first stages now of establishing footholds in space for human habitation where people can live and work productively.

In the next century, people will be living in permanent bases on the Moon and perhaps on Mars. As has happened throughout the history of human exploration, the people who go to these places will bring something of their religion and their culture with them.

Some things will change and some will remain immutable. I am proud of my religious heritage, and am expressing this pride by my choice of objects to accompany me on my flight.

I am touched by this letter because it makes the point that the further out into space you go, the further into the unknown you go, the further into the future you go, the more you want to feel a sense of kinship, a sense of connection, a sense of continuity with the past. Because, otherwise, if you don't have that, then you become like a piece of flotsam, floating up there, unrelated to everything around you. There is very little gravity up there in space, and so people float up there when they leave the spacecraft unless they have a rope or a line to keep them connected to it while they go exploring. And that is what the tallit and the Torah and the Jewish way of life are to us ~ they are lifelines, ropes that keep us grounded and that keep us connected to the past as we venture into the unknown future.

So think of it: one of these days there will be colonies out there in space, and people will go there to farm and to live. And there will be tours from Earth to visit these places. I can't wait till I am able to buy a ticket on a space shuttle and go to visit. I am already talking to our travel agent about a synagogue-sponsored tour to outer space. And I have no doubt that when we get there, and when they give us a tour of the place, there will be homes with mezuzot, and there will be Jews with tallitot, and, if it is a real Jewish community, there will be two synagogues there ~ one a break-off from the other.

And in both, the people will be praying to the God whom we Jews call רִבּוֹן כָּל הָעוֹלָמִים (*Ribon Kol Ha-Olamim.*) [It is one of the wonders of the Jewish tradition that centuries ago, Jews called God not only רִבּוֹנוֹ שֶׁל עוֹלָם (*Ribono shel olam*) ~ Master of the universe ~ but רִבּוֹן כָּל הָעוֹלָמִים (*Ribon Kol Ha-Olamim*), which means Master of *all* the universes, Lord of all the cosmos, for that is what God is.]

And in both synagogues they will be praying what it says in the Kedushah:

נְקַדֵּשׁ אֶת־שִׁמְךָ בָּעוֹלָם, כְּשֵׁם שֶׁמַּקְדִּישִׁים
אוֹתוֹ בִּשְׁמֵי מָרוֹם

Nikadesh et shimkha ba-olam kishem shemak'dishim
oto bishmey marom

May you, down there on earth, hallow God's name
just as it is sanctified up here in the heights above.

That line has new meaning for us in this generation, for we have been privileged to get a closer glimpse into the workings of the cosmos than those that came before us. And who can fail to be awed, who can not be moved, who cannot feel the wonder and the glory and the majesty and the mystery of the constellations and the planets when you see them up close as our generation can?

And in both of these synagogues they will pray:

עֹשֶׂה שָׁלוֹם בִּמְרוֹמָיו, הוּא יַעֲשֶׂה שָׁלוֹם עָלֵינוּ.

Oseh shalom bimromav hu ya-aseh shalom aleynu.

May the One who makes the harmony of the heavens
bring peace and harmony to all who dwell on Earth.

And may this prayer come true.

Knots: A Sermon for Sh'lah
Shamai Kanter

When we cross our arms, we participate in re-enacting one of the most important discoveries in human history. It is interlacing, something children probably discovered but only an adult came to appreciate. Interlacing is the basic idea behind the weaving of baskets and cloth, braiding hair or rope, of all kinds of knotting and tying. It is one of the basic discoveries of human culture.

Indeed, if the historians and anthropologists are correct when they tell us that we were food-gatherers before we were hunters or farmers, then the first human tool may not have been the axe or hammer, or knife or spear. It may have been a basket, made for the collection and carrying of food.

Now we are finding out that there's a deeper meaning to the acts of knotting and weaving. Those simple actions are a clue to a deeper understanding of the universe. There is a branch of mathematics called knot theory. It deals with the mathematics behind different kinds of knots, and it enables us to understand things like the way complex molecules develop. If you've ever seen microscopic photos of something like DNA, which is the basis for the way living cells reproduce themselves, you know that DNA loops around in the shape of a complex kind of knot. With a little bit of DNA identified, the mathematics behind the knot helps researchers predict what the rest of the DNA will be.

Even more than that: (here I'm moving, with apology, into a field I know nothing about) the cutting edge of theoretical physics nowadays is something called string theory. It is a way of understanding the energy that holds atoms together, or is electricity, or gravity, not in terms of waves or pulses, but as strings. It is a theory of the way all energy is organized, from within the atoms to beyond the galaxies.

So if you want to know the secret of the universe, the hidden pattern behind everything, the secret meaning of its structure, you could say that reality is composed of strings and knots ~ or more precisely, the mathematics behind strings and knots.

All of this casts some new light on a famous passage of the Torah. We read it this morning as the last paragraph of the Torah reading, but the rabbis liked it so much that they included it in the daily service for every morning and evening:

> *Adonai spoke to Moses, saying "Speak to the children of Israel, and bid them make tzitzit (knotted tassels) on the corners of their garments throughout their generations...And it shall be to you for a tzitzit, so that you look upon it and remember all the commandments of Adonai, and do them ... and be holy to your God." (Numbers 15:37-41)*

The knots and tassels serve as a reminder not of the pattern behind the physical universe, but of the structure of moral and religious commandments that relate us to God. And they do it through the mathematical meaning of the צִיצָת (*tzitzit*).

Those of you who are wearing tallitot, and whose eyesight is good enough, can count the windings in each of the four sections. Notice that they are all different: 7, and 8, and 11, and 13. They add up to the number 39. Since each Hebrew letter has a numerical meaning, too (א / *aleph* = 1, ב / *bet* = 2, all the way up to ת / *tav* = 400), 39 translates into the number phrase יְיָ אֶחָד (*Adonai Ehad*) ~ Adonai is One.

The word צִיצָת (*tzitzit*)itself has a numerical value:
צ (*tzadi*) + י (*yod*) + צ (*tzadi*) + י (*yod*) + ת (*tav*)
add up to 600. If you look at your tzitzit again, you'll see that it has 8 strings plus 5 knots. So the sum total is 613, the number associated with the mitzvot, the commandments of the Torah.

So the mathematical meaning of the knotted tassels of the tallit is clear: the meaning of the universe lies in the One God and the structure of moral/religious commandments that tie us to God.

There's one more comment I want to share with you. This is the season most young people choose for their weddings. This week our congregation has been celebrating a wedding....

What's the common phrase we use to describe getting married? That's right; it is "tying the knot." I hope you now realize that there may be a lot more to that idiom than you realized before. It is not just that two people become bonded to each other in marriage, that their lives are linked together. When they marry, they have the awareness that they've discovered, through their relationship, something of the meaning of life. They have found part of the concealed, spiritual pattern of existence.

Their relationship represents the only way the Bible found to describe the connection between God and the Jewish people:

> *I will betroth you to Me forever. I will betroth you*
> *to Me through righteousness and justice, through*
> *love and mercy. I will betroth you to Me through*
> *faithfulness, and you will know, will love Adonai.*
>
> *(Hosea 2:21-22)*

In Jewish marriage, people not only link themselves to each other. They also interweave their lives with the lives of their families. They tie themselves to the life of a community and its destiny. And they bind themselves in relationship with God. Because of that weaving, we not only wish joy to our חָתָן (*hatan*) and כַּלָה (*kallah*), we also share in their joy ourselves.

"And the tzitzit shall be for you"
A Bar Mitzvah D'var Torah
Alon Futterman

This Shabbat I shall put on my tallit for the first time when I am called to the Torah as a bar mitzvah. The mitzvah of צִיצִת (*tzitzit*) appears at the end of the parashah, שְׁלַח־לְךָ (*Sh'lah Lekha*).

What should it mean to me? In Menahot 48b we are taught, "This mitzvah is equal to the weight of all the other mitzvot." Is it possible that this simple mitzvah is of greater significance than all the mitzvot we are commanded to observe with regard to other human beings, not to mention all those that pertain to our relationship with God? The Talmud offers the explanation that seeing (the tzitzit) leads to remembering (all the mitzvot), which in turn leads to their observance.

Rashi brings a symbolic insight into this matter based on gematriya. He notes that the Hebrew word צִיצָת (*tzitzit*) has the numerical value of 600, which when combined with the number of knots (5) and fringes (8) found on each corner of the tallit, gives us the number of mitzvot (613) that we are commanded to observe. He suggests that this is how we are to understand "and when you see it you will remember all of God's mitzvot." Perhaps this is what I am supposed to think about when I put on my tallit.

The verses of Psalm 104:1-2 are traditionally recited before one says the בְּרָכָה (*b'rakhah*) for wearing the tallit: "Adonai, my God, You are very great; You are clothed in glory and majesty, wrapped in a robe of light." I understand this to mean that just as the King above wears special royal clothes made from the light that He created, I can imitate God by wearing a garment ~ the tallit ~ commanded by the Torah, which is God's light to us. Of course, there are implications here as well, beyond just the specific mitzvah of tzitzit. We have learned from the rabbis about all kinds of mitzvot that constitute imitating God's ways, such as בִּקוּר חוֹלִים (*bikkur holim*), for God visited the ailing Avraham after his circumcision. Perhaps this is what I am supposed to think about when I put on my tallit:

> "How precious is your loving kindness, Adonai;
> humanity finds shelter in the shadow of Your wings"
> (Psalm 36:8).

These words appear as part of the כַּוָּנָה (*kavannah*) that follows the בְּרָכָה (*b'rakhah*) for putting on the tallit. It conjures up the image of God as שְׁכִינָה (*Shekhinah*) who, like a mother bird, protects her young beneath her wings just as she once took them out of Egypt on the wings of eagles (Exodus 19:4). I already associate such feelings of love and protection with the tallit from all those mornings I stood beneath my father's tallit as the כּוֹהֲנִים (*kohanim*) recited the priestly benediction. Perhaps this is what I am supposed to think about when I put on my tallit.

The very option of choosing what to think about will help me to fulfill the meaning of the words, "And the tzitzit shall be for you," so that each time I wear the tallit will become a personally meaningful moment in my life.

Curbing Your Lustful Eyes
Pinhas H. Peli

Tzitzit—The old *Jewish Encyclopedia* sends us to "see Fringes." The more recent *Encyclopedia Judaica* has this to say: "name of the tassels attached to the four corners of special garments worn by men in fulfillment of the biblical commandment in Numbers 15:37-41 and Deuteronomy 22:12. It has been suggested that the *tzitzit* served as a talisman (amulet) or that it was instituted in order to distinguish between male and female garments, which were very similar in biblical times."

The *tanaim*, the leading rabbinic sages of the early centuries of the common era, seem to be far more enamored with the subject than the modern encyclopedists: "Whoever fulfils the precept of tzitzit is to be considered as if he has fulfilled the entire Torah..." "Whosoever fulfils the precept of tzitzit, Scripture looks upon him as if he were in the company of the *Shechina* (the holy presence of God)..."

"The commandment of tzitzit outweighs all other commandments of the Torah" (Sifrei 15, 39: TB Nedarim 25a, and many parallel sources).

If these exalting statements were not enough, the passage in Numbers 15:37-41, which contains the commandment to put tassels, entwined with a thread of purple, on the four-cornered garments, became at a very early stage in the formation of Jewish liturgy part of the twice-daily recitation of the "declaration of faith" (Mishna Tamid 5,I). To this very day, it is recited at the centre of the synagogue service together with the other two parts of the *Sh'ma*, which tell about the love of God and acceptance of His kingship (Deut. 6:4-9) and about the fulfillment of His commandments (ibid. 11:13-21).

What is it that gave tzitzit this central position in the thought and practice of early Judaism? It could hardly be because of its being an amulet or even a distinguishing mark between male and female garments. In fact, Torah itself explains the purpose of the fringes. They are to be in front of the eyes as a constant reminder to observe "all the commandments of the Lord." Looking at them will cause you not to follow your own wandering desires and fancies but to obey all the commandments, in order to become holy for the sake of God.

Absent-minded and forgetful as people are, the extra fringes on the garment which they wear will remind them of their duty, not letting their mind stray in pursuit of their hearts' desires and lustful eyes. Elaborating on this obvious rationale for tzitzit, the rabbis offer a beautiful explanation on how the tzitzit accomplish this task. It is by way of the psychological impact resulting from a train of associations in color.

"The purple of the tzitzit resembles the ocean, the ocean resembles the heavens, the heavens bring to mind the throne of glory." *U're'item oto u'zchartem et kol mitzvot hashem* ~ "and you shall look at it (at the fringe) and be reminded of all the commandments of the Lord." The word "it" *(oto)* could also mean "Him" (there being no neutral gender in Hebrew). Hence, looking at the color of the purple thread, one can behold Him, as it were, and thereby be reminded of His commandments.

The tzitzit are not the only reminders of the commandments. There are other signs and symbols (tefillin, mezuzah, etc.) that fill this purpose. There must be something special about tzitzit that is not found in all the other reminders.

The rabbinic explanation for the inclusion of tzitzit as one of the *Sh'ma* passages is that it cites the exodus from Egyptian bondage, which must be mentioned every day. A person cannot declare the kingship of God, nor accept obedience to His commandments (the first two passages of the *Sh'ma*), without declaring at the same time his being a free person thanks to God having delivered him from bondage.

The event of the Exodus is cited in other biblical passages as well. Why then was this one selected to be put in such a prominent place? Because it contains also the teaching that love of God (first passage of *Sh'ma)* or obedience to Him expecting reward or out of fear (second passage) are not enough. The love of God and the fulfillment of His commandments must have a purpose. The purpose is spelled out in the passage regarding tzitzit: "And you shall do the commandments in order to become holy to your God." While God *is* holy, the commandments help us *become* holy, as we were told earlier (Leviticus 19:1): "Ye shall *become* holy, because I, the Lord your God, am holy." This requires love of God together with the purposeful fulfillment of the commandments as free people.

The blue or purple *(tekhelet)* thread in tzitzit emphasizes this last point. Purple was known in the ancient world as a typical royal color. The prophet Ezekiel (23:6) mentions the princes and nobles who wore garments of tekhelet. Archeological findings from the ancient Near East show princes and noblemen wearing garments edged with tassels of knitted fringes. Wearing tzitzit is thus a sign of nobility and royalty. Who attains nobility? He who is not enslaved to anyone, nor to his own blind desires, but accepts voluntarily the "yoke of the kingship of

God," obedience to His commandments, and strives to a life of holiness.

Tzitzit are not a talisman, an amulet to guard the person who wears them from demons and evil spirits. Reminding one of his nobility, they *do* keep him away from evil, in the sense of *noblesse oblige*. To demonstrate this function of tzitzit as representing the inner conscience of the religious person, the following story appears in most of the talmudic and midrashic sources dealing with the importance of tzitzit. We copy it verbatim from the Babylonian Talmud tractate Menahot, p.44a (Soncino English translation):

> Once a man who was very scrupulous about the precept of tzitzit heard of a certain harlot in one of the towns of the sea who accepted four hundred dinars for her hire. He sent her the sum and appointed a day with her. When the day arrived he came and waited at the door, and her maid came and told her, 'That man who sent you 400 dinars is here and waiting at the door,' to which she replied, 'Let him come in.'
>
> When he came in she prepared for him seven beds, six of silver and one of gold, and between one bed and the other there were steps of silver, but the last were of gold. She then went up to the top bed and lay down upon it naked. He too went up after her in his desire to sit naked with her, when all of a sudden the four fringes of his garment struck him across the face; whereupon

he slipped off and sat upon the ground. She
also slipped off and sat upon the ground and
said, 'By the Roman Capitol (a form of oath;
according to Rashi: By the head of Rome,
referring to the Emperor), I will not leave you
alone until you tell me what blemish you found
in me.' 'By the Temple,' he replied, 'never have
I seen a woman as beautiful as you are; but
there is one precept which the Lord our God has
commanded us; it is called tzitzit, and with
regard to it the expression *I am the Lord your God*
is twice written (Num. 15:41), signifying, I am
He who will exact punishment in the future and
I am He who will give reward in the future.
Now, the tzitzit appeared to me as four witnesses
testifying against me.'

She said, 'I will not leave you until you tell me
your name, the name of your town, the name of
your teacher, the name of your school in which
you study your Torah.' He wrote all this down
and handed it to her. Thereupon she arose and
divided her estate into three parts; one third for
the government, one third to be distributed
among the poor, and one third she took with her
in her hand. The bedclothes, however, she
retained.

She then came to the school of Rab Hiyya, and
said to him, 'Master, give instructions, that they
make me a proselyte.' 'My daughter,' he replied,
'perhaps you have set your eyes on one of the
disciples?' She thereupon took out the slip and

handed it to him. 'Go,' said he, 'and enjoy your acquisition.' The very bedclothes which she spread for him for an illicit purpose she now spread out for him lawfully.

'This,' Rabbi Nathan, who tells the story, concludes, 'is the reward of tzitzit in this world, and as for its reward in the future world I know not how great it is.'"

The Fringed Garment:
The Mitzvah of Tzitzit
Hershel Matt

One of the most conspicuous signs of Jewish worship is the tallit: the shawl with fringes (צִיצִת - *tzitzit*) at its corners, worn by men during morning prayer, whether in public or in private. Commanded twice in the Torah, included prominently in the prayer book as the concluding portion of the Sh'ma Yisrael, cherished through the ages, observed by the faithful Jewish man on every single day ~ this mitzvah is one of the most familiar of the commandments of the Torah, and one of the most important. Indeed, some of the sages taught: "Whoever fulfills the single mitzvah of צִיצִת (*tzitzit*) is as if he had fulfilled all of the mitzvot."

What is the meaning of this mitzvah of the fringed garment, and why should it be considered so important?

The key to the answer is to be found in verses 37 through 41 in the fifteenth chapter of the Book of Numbers (Bemidbar), fourth of the Five Books of the Torah:

> *Adonai spoke to Moses, saying: Speak to the Children of Israel and instruct them to make for themselves fringes on the corners of their garments throughout the generations; let them attach a cord of blue to the fringe at each corner. That shall be your fringe; look at it and recall all the commandments of Adonai and observe them, so that you do not follow your heart and eyes in your lustful urge. Thus shall you be reminded to observe all My commandments and to be holy to your God. I Adonai am your God, who brought you out of the land of Egypt to be your God: I Adonai, your God.*

From this passage, we see that the purpose of the צִיצָת (*tzitzit*) is the purpose of all the commandments: to aid Israel in becoming holy. To be holy ~ in Hebrew, קָדוֹשׁ (*kadosh*) ~ involves both a "separation from" and a "dedication to": a separation from that which is idolatrous, spiritually contaminating, morally degrading; and a dedication to that which is godly, spiritually purifying, and morally elevating.

And from this passage we also see that living a life hallowed by such separation and such dedication was God's whole purpose in redeeming Israel from Egypt. Previous to the Exodus, every human being, of course, had been created in God's image; every human society had caught at least a glimpse of God's standard for human justice and love. Yet human society had rarely risen above the pagan; the image of God again and again had been blurred and tarnished, defaced, and at times almost effaced. So God now saw fit to redeem Israel from Egyptian bondage and to speak to Israel at Sinai ~ revealing God's will and word and way for man, in far greater measure and in far more detail than heretofore; offering surer guidance, richer resources, greater help for living the life of holiness.

From this passage we see, furthermore, that God's act of deliverance is the very basis for the commandments; the Exodus is proclaimed to be the evidence of God's transcendent power, of God's sovereign authority, of God's everpresence, of God's concern. "I, YHVH, am Adonai," God is saying: therefore, obey Me. I have the right to command you, because I am the One who rules: I choose to command you, because I am the One who cares.

Every faithful Jew acknowledges these truths. Every faithful Jew knows that the Exodus from Egypt and the Giving of the Torah-and-commandments are the foundation of his life. Yet every faithful Jew knows also that Israel neglects the purpose of the Exodus and forsakes the commandments, that the Children of Israel forget, fall short, and falter. And so every faithful Jew knows that he must wear the fringes, for the fringes serve as a visible reminder of the commandments of Adonai; they serve as a spur to holy deeds and holy words and even holy thoughts. (In olden times one of the threads was blue, reminiscent of the heavens, and thus of the heavenly throne of the Holy God.) Seeing the fringe, a Jew remembers the commandments; remembering, he strives to do them. All three steps are important: the seeing, the remembering, and the doing.

Yes, the tallit, when regularly and reverently worn, can strengthen our will and replenish our resources for resisting the temptation to do evil.

And this temptation is ever present: the heart constantly prompts to evil and promises reward; the eyes continually see and indeed seek out opportunities for evil; the limbs hasten to execute our evil desire. Again and again we are tempted to use our powers of body, mind, and heart in the service of "another" rather than in the service of the "One." We are easily seduced to prostitute our gifts and faculties, to be unfaithful to the Loving One who betrothed us to Himself at the Exodus, who wedded us to Himself at Sinai. (No wonder that, when the fringed outer garment had to give way to a special fringed shawl used at the time of prayer alone, a fringed undergarment was then developed ~ so that one might still bear on his person throughout the day the reminder of God's commandments.)

And yet, though the temptation to sin is always present and the warning to resist is always present, though the yoke of the commandments is always upon us and the urge to break it off is always within us, the Jew-with-fringes is not terrified or overwhelmed by the burden. He is not crushed or cowed. For he ever recalls that the One who commands is also the One who loves; that, indeed, God's very commands are tokens of God's love ~ designed to help and guide, to strengthen and protect, to yield true happiness and blessing. The sacred duties and holy obligation are holy opportunities and sacred privilege as well. They are rungs of a ladder lovingly extended by God to us, God's children, enabling us lovingly to progress on the holy ascent. (No wonder that many worshippers kiss the fringed reminders of the commandments whenever the word צִיצָת - *tzitzit* is uttered.)

But the progress is not continuous; the journey is not always straight upward. The ascent at times appears too steep, the climb too tiring, the struggle endless. One wants to forget about duty, task, and obligation. One feels a need to shut out the world ~ with its temptations and tribulations, its tricks and its traps and its troubles, a need not slowly to climb and to trudge but to flee and to fly; a need to take cover under the sheltering wings of our loving Father in heaven (the Hebrew word כָּנָף - *kanaf* means both "corner of the garment" and "wing"), a need to seek not God's approbation of what we have done or earned or been, but God's forgiving acceptance in spite of what we have failed to do or earn or be; a need to come as close as is given to man to come to the pure and purifying שְׁכִינָה (*Shekhinah*) of God's presence. (Perhaps that is why men cover their head and shield their eyes as they enwrap themselves in the tallit.)

Nevertheless, this time withdrawal from the world for the sake of worship ~ of uttering our word to God and of listening to God's word to us ~ must be followed by a return to the world, so that we may seek to carry out the word we have received and accepted anew. For the world is still the world of scattered Israel, not yet restored to Zion; it is the world of fragmented mankind, still unredeemed. (That is why the fringes of the four corners are gathered together as we pray for the ingathering of redemption.) The commandments continue to be upon us and with us each day of our life, till the day of our death. (A man is buried in his tallit ~ though then the fringe is concealed or removed.)

We have discovered the meaning ~ or some aspects, at least, of the meaning ~ of the mitzvah of צִיצִת (*tzitzit*); the function it performs, the reminder it provides, the strength it affords, the purification it accomplishes, the protection it gives. And yet none of this comes automatically; the mere presence of the fringes on the garment, the mere wearing of the garment on the body, the mere accompanying recital of the words, the mere presence of a Jew-in-name standing garbed-in-fringes for prayer-in-words ~ all this guarantees nothing at all. (Indeed, if the mere externals of religion were believed to guarantee results, our ritual and worship would be little better than primitive magic and pagan superstition. After all, heathens, too, have been known to wear fringes on their garments.) The value of the mitzvah of צִיצָת (*tzitzit*) lies in a radically different understanding of the ritual object and its use; the tallit must be worn in the true spirit of a mitzvah; wherein a Jew stands in readiness to hear the word that God proclaims, to accept the task that God assigns, to fulfill the deed that God prescribes. Only then is he enabled to receive, here and hereafter, the blessing God provides.

Some Further Interpretations and Rules of Tzitzit

Since the chief biblical passage concerning the fringes refers to them as a reminder of all the commandments, the mitzvah has been interpreted to yield the number 613, which is the traditional sum of all the commandments: the numerical value of the letters in the Hebrew word צִיצָת (*tzitzit*) ~

צ (*tzadi*), י (*yod*), צ (*tzadi*), י (*yod*), ת (*tav*) amounts to 600, the four strands in each corner, doubled over, yield 8 more; the five knots dividing the sets of coils yield the final 5. The fringes in each corner are wound in coils, as follows: coils of 7 and 8, totaling 15, whose Hebrew equivalent is י,ה (*yod, heh*) ~ the first two letters of God's special name; a coil of 11, whose Hebrew equivalent is ו,ה (*vav, heh*) ~ the last two letters of that name; and a final coil of 13, equaling the numerical value of א,ח,ד (*alef, chet,* and *dalet*) ~ the letters of the Hebrew word אֶחָד (*echad*), "one."

Since the biblical passage under discussion includes the phrase "you shall look at it" (the fringe), the dominant view in the tradition has been that this commandment applies only in daytime. The tallit is worn, therefore, only in the morning. It is also worn on Kol Nidre eve, however, since that service commences while it is still daylight. The dominant view has also held that this mitzvah applies only to men, since women are exempt from positive mitzvot that involve a time factor. Although the mitzvah is obligatory only upon those who have reached the age of mitzvot (bar mitzvah), it is appropriate for minors also to wear צִיצָת (*tzitzit*) for the sake of training in the mitzvot. The blue dye for coloring one thread of each corner fringe was obtained in ancient times from a mollusk called *hilazon*. When this mollusk became extinct, or when its identity was no longer certain, the practice of using a blue thread was discontinued, since it was felt that the exact hue could no longer be produced. In some subsequent eras, however ~ and even in our own ~ some authorities have zealously sought and claim to have found the correct species of mollusk, and have therefore revived the original practice. [The blue and white colors of the flag of the State of Israel ~ formerly the Zionist flag ~ have their origin in the blue and white of the צִיצִת (*tzitzit*)]. The one other biblical passage referring to the mitzvah of the fringes is the twelfth verse of the twenty-second chapter of the fifth of the Five Books of the Torah, the Book of D'varim (Deuteronomy): "You shall make tassels on the four corners of the garment with which you cover yourself."

Some Suggestions for the Proper Observance of the Mitzvah of Tzitzit

Provide yourself with your own tallit for use in public worship (even if your synagogue provides a tallit for each worshipper) and for use in private worship, at home or away from home. Make sure that it is large enough to cover most of your body, and that it is beautiful enough to be considered by you as an adornment. Provide yourself with a tallit bag, also. Consider using two tallitot: one for weekdays, and one for Shabbat and Yom Tov. When tefillin are worn, the tallit is put on first and removed last. Before donning the tallit, pause for a moment in prayerful preparation for performing the mitzvah; pronounce the בְּרָכָה (*b'rakhah*) reverently; enwrap yourself in the manner of a shawl rather than of a scarf; add a further word of prayer. [The בְּרָכָה (*b'rakhah*) and suggested meditations are found at the beginning of most siddurim.]

During the בְּרָכָה (*b'rakhah*) before the Sh'ma, gather the four corner fringes (if possible, as you say the words "gather us in shalom from the four corners of the earth"). Hold the gathered fringes throughout the Sh'ma; during the third portion of the Sh'ma, look at the fringes each time you pronounce the word צִיצָת (*tzitzit*) ~ perhaps actually kissing them. Release them after the Sh'ma is concluded. At the conclusion of your morning prayer, remove the tallit gently, reluctantly; fold it neatly; and return it carefully to the tallit bag. Keep your tallit in an appropriate place. Check periodically to see whether your tallit needs to be laundered, or to have its fringes replaced, or to be entirely replaced. [New צִיצָת (*tzitzit*) as well as new tallitot can be obtained at all Jewish book stores; there you can also receive help in inserting the new tzitzit, as you can also from your rabbi, cantor, Hebrew school principal or teacher, and shamash.] Although not considered to be holy in the same sense as books or parchments containing God's name, fringes or tallitot, when no longer usable, should not be crudely discarded but should rather be put aside for eventual burial in cemetery. (Your synagogue has a place for keeping such objects until burial.) If you are gifted artistically (or have a friend who is), consider the possibility of having your tallit and tallit bag hand designed or hand-made. (No fringes other than the corner fringe are necessary; and as for the stripes in the tallit, there is no requirement concerning their size, color or arrangement, or even their presence.) Leave instructions that when you die you wish to be buried in your tallit. Consider giving a tallit as a gift ~ to a friend whose tallit needs replacing, or to one who owns no tallit but would cherish one or would at least consider using it. (It is a worthy custom for the bride or her family to give the groom a tallit as a wedding present.)

If you do not at present wear the under-tallit (called *arba kanfot* or *tallit katan* or tzitzit) ~ and even if you have never done so, consider seriously the possibility of beginning to do so - perhaps along with the other men or boys in your family, at least on an experimental basis of, say, one month or one year.

Check whether your synagogue provides tallitot in sufficient number for all worshippers who do not bring their own; and whether it provides proper care for the tallitot it owns ~ including storing, inspection, laundering, and replacement. Offer your assistance in connection with this mitzvah.

My Grandfather's Tallis
Steven Carr Reuben

My grandfather's tallis was a wondrous thing to
behold. I knew that it carried with it some secret
magic powers, else why would he wrap himself
completely in it from head to foot, burying his head
and swaying slowly back and forth while uttering
strange, mystical sounds and words in a secret
foreign language? My grandfather's tallis had powers
that I could only dream of ~ what mystical
incantations he intoned in those dark secret private
moments I could only guess, and my fertile childhood
imagination wove mysteries and fantasies by the
score. My grandfather's tallis was a world unto itself.
It was an enormous sacred tent spread over the holy
sparks of his piety, sparks that cast their brilliance
upon my own eager and curious eyes each time I
would gaze upon it.

My grandfather's tallis had a smell all its own ~ an old-world aroma that conjured up visions of a sea of old men with long beards and dark clothes gathered together in huddled close-knit synagogues, attempting through their prayers to bring the Messiah. My grandfather's tallis appeared to my childish eyes like a great Superman cape allowing my grandfather to leap spiritual heights with a single bound and soar up, up, and away into a world of sacred light.

In truth, I only saw my grandfather's tallis once or twice a year, when after celebrating with my family in our Reform synagogue on Rosh Hashanah I would eagerly go with my grandfather on the second day of the holiday to his Orthodox shul near the beach in Venice. There I entered a strange and wonderful world of rooms filled with taleisim just like grandfather's, each concealing another older man rocking and swaying to the unintelligible, yet somehow meaningful rhythm of Hebrew incantations.

There was something about sitting in that sanctuary with my grandfather that always sent shivers down my spine and filled me with a sense of awe and wonder. It seemed I could sit for hours listening to the music of a language I didn't understand, yet feeling its spiritual power and potency to the very marrow of my being. And of course, there was my favorite pastime during all those hours, sitting, watching and listening. My favorite pastime naturally was playing with my grandfather's צִיצִת (*tzitzit*).

What could possibly be more wonderful than those dancing, knotted tattered fringes that kept beat with the chant of the hazzan and the march of the Torahs down the aisle? What could possibly be more wondrous than curling my fingers around those mystical fringes and wondering all along at what hidden significance they must surely possess?

There is a story told about the Baal Shem Tov, the 18th-century founder of Hasidism in Eastern Europe, that his disciples could learn more by watching the fringes of his tallis than most others could learn from a week immersed in the study of the Talmud. As I thought this year about the power hidden in my grandfather's tallis, I understood what the Baal Shem Tov meant. To me, my grandfather's tallis was a symbol of continuity, a symbol of strength, a physical, tactile artifact of ages gone by and ancient wisdoms revealed.

As I look back on those formative experiences of my youth, those precious encounters with the mysteries of what seemed to me to represent the half-forgotten memories of an ancient people, I appreciate so profoundly how important artifacts and symbols are in our lives. Indeed, our lives are virtually filled with symbols and artifacts. The heirloom passed down from grandmother to mother to daughter; a picture that hangs on the wall of a grandparent or great-grandparent that you never knew, yet still feel in some way is an important part of your own past; the Shabbat candlesticks that your mother blessed; perhaps a Bible with a few family names and dates written in the center, that sits on your shelf; a vase that belonged to a great aunt, or an antique that you rescued one hot summer afternoon from a garage sale down the block.

Yes, artifacts do fill up our lives, reminding us of cherished moments of the past. Like the flower from your first date that, pressed between the pages of a picture album, conjures up feelings of excitement, the thrill of a first kiss, a first rented tuxedo and a night of acting as grown-up as possible, so the sacred remnants of our Jewish past remain precious and meaningful in potential today. Life is not inherently filled with meaning ~ it is only filled with opportunities to create meaning. We are a people of memory, and I recall sitting at the feet of Israel's greatest Talmudic scholar, Rabbi Adin Steinsaltz, as he told an eager group of 15 Jewish American college students, of which I was one many years ago, that "the homeland of the Jew is history."

We say in our tradition, "Rabbi Hillel says," and not "said," to impress upon us the reality that the words, mitzvah-experiences, and opportunities of the Jewish past are equally alive and present for us today. We either take them and embrace them for our own to transcend the mundane nature of our everyday lives and transform them into things of beauty, purpose and significance ~ or we don't. Either way, it is up to us. To some, my grandfather's tallis may be just a piece of cloth with some strings attached, but how foolish I would be if that were all it was. My grandfather's tallis represents the myriad ritual and symbolic opportunities that fill our lives each day and virtually overflow with the richness of religious promise and possibility.

Today is one of those days of opportunity. This very day, this new beginning, this new year, is yet another precious opportunity to create purpose, spiritual satisfaction, and meaning in your life. You can take this very day, with all its resplendent symbols, rituals, prayers, songs, and stories and let it inspire you to discover the you that longs to burst forth into the light of the new year. Each of us needs moments in our lives, spaces in our hectic daily schedules to sit back, take a deep breath, and rest our over-burdened bodies and spirits. We need these moments of spiritual refreshment and reflection to take stock of our lives, reassess our personal goals and desires, and rededicate our energies to the fulfillment of our own life dreams.

I remember hearing a famous artist describe the process of his painting. At one point he described how there comes a point in his painting when he must stop, step back from the canvas, and simply do nothing: that crucial artistic moment, when one more stroke makes the difference between a creation of beauty, and just another painting. Rosh Hashanah is our time to step back from the canvas of our lives and see, really see, the picture we have created all year. Today, now, is the very moment of decision making. Now is the moment when you can choose that one stroke, that one decision that you have needed to make in your life, to turn it into a creation of beauty, poetry, splendor.

The legendary Russian dancer, Nyjinsky, was renowned throughout the world for his uncanny ability to leap during performances in such a way as to hang suspended in the air as if forever. When asked how he accomplished this remarkable artistic feat, he smiled and responded, "I simply leap, and pause." Today is your opportunity to leap and pause. Take the chance that breaking away from old patterns can free you forever from the chains of your own past. Leap, leap out into the unknown. Leap to heights you never reached before and pause. Pause to gaze around you at the view from a new height, a new perspective on life and its potential that will fill you with the excitement of a new discovery of self.

Anais Nin once wrote, "Life shrinks or expands in proportion to one's courage." Today is the anniversary in Jewish tradition of the birthday of the world, a time when the universe paused, and the earth leapt into creative being. As we celebrate today the power of a world in constant creation, a world engaged in daily evolution, change, becoming, you and I can embrace this as a personal model for our own life-process. We, too, are in constant creation; you and I are a world all our own engaged in daily evolution, changing, growing, discovering, becoming. But unlike the world around us, our inner world, the private universe of our being, dances to a rhythm of our own design.

You paint the picture of your life; you determine whether it's filled with brush strokes of vivid color and tender hue, or is just another painting. You determine the music that plays the melody of your life. You write the score, day in and day out, adding notes of harmony or discord. "Not he is great who can alter matter, but he who can alter any state of mind," said Emerson. Indeed, that does take courage.

It is not always easy to let go of the past that has become so very comfortable. So what if the bars obscure the view of the beauty that lies outside the cage, at least it's safe in here. At least I know the routine, I know what to expect, I don't have to face the anxiety of the unknown. Ah, but think of all we miss when we fail to embrace the courage to change, to leap and pause. Shakespeare in Hamlet reminds us so profoundly, "We know what we are, but we know not what we may be."

"What we may be," lies locked away in the future. "What we may be," depends on our willingness to take that leap of faith, to discover courage in the words of our high holiday liturgy that impel us to change, move on, emulate the ongoing creation of the world as co-partners with the underlying spirituality that fills the universe, create meaning, say "Yes, there is a purpose to my life, and I will make it so."

On this Rosh Hashanah, this second chance for change, this birthday of a new year and a new you, I ask, "Why not you?" Why not you, watching the morning mist rise over the mountains of Scotland? Why not you, catching a play on the London stage, standing on top of the Eiffel Tower and gazing directly at the Mona Lisa in Paris? Why not you, walking the Great Wall in China, riding the Bullet Train in Japan, visiting the outback of Australia to catch a glimpse of a kangaroo? Why not you, sailing the canals of Venice on a gondola with someone you love, catching a sunrise from the top of Masada and gazing down to the austere beauty of the Dead Sea?

And why not you, embracing the Jewish ideal of תִּקּוּן עוֹלָם (*tikkun olam*), taking part in the life task of making whole the broken fragments of the world? Why not you, inventing a new product, creating a new idea, changing someone's life or inspiring another through your own inspiration? Why not you, being happy, joyful, filling your life with loving, giving, sharing, caring, touching, laughter and tenderness? Why not you, wealthy, successful, satisfied, productive, creative, enthusiastic, courageous, energetic, purposeful?

Today is a day for saying, "Why not you!" There is no such thing in anyone's life as an unimportant day. Every day counts. Every one is yet another chance to say, "Why not me?" Time is not measured by the passing of years, but by what one does, what one experiences, what one achieves. Do great things this year and your life will be great. This is our new year, our new beginning, our time of choosing who and what we will be in the year to come.

But in truth, the "year to come" is but a fantasy in our mind, a projection of the future as unreal, and out of our control, as the lives of our children or grandchildren. What is real, what we can control, what we must control is today. Today is all we ever have. This very day, and this day only, to do with as we choose. Time is the inexplicable raw material of everything. With it, all is possible; without it, nothing. The supply of time is truly a daily miracle, an affair of astonishment when one examines it. You wake up in the morning, and lo!, your purse is magically filled with 24 hours of the unmanufactured tissue of the universe of your life.

It is yours; it is the most precious of possessions; no one can take it away from you; it is unstealable. No one receives either more or less than you receive. In the realm of time, there is no aristocracy of wealth and no aristocracy of intellect. Genius is never rewarded by even an extra hour a day. And there is no punishment. Waste your infinitely precious commodity as much as you will, and the supply will never be withheld from you. Moreover, you cannot draw on the future. It's impossible to get into debt. You can only waste the passing moment. You cannot waste tomorrow. It is kept for you. You cannot waste the next hour, it is kept for you.

This truly is one of the greatest of miracles, is it not? You have these 24 hours of daily time to live. If one cannot arrange that an income of 24 hours shall exactly cover all proper items of expenditure, one does muddle one's whole life indefinitely. We shall never have any more time. We have and have always had all the time there is.

Today, I remember my grandfather's tallis and I smile. That tallis reminds me each year, each holiday, that the meaning that exists in the world is the meaning I bring to the world. One tallis, one old man, one model, one symbol, one artifact, and one changed life.

What will you do with your time this year? What will you do with your time today? Why not you, making a difference in the lives of others? The Talmud teaches that the story of creation in Genesis begins with the creation of one man in order to teach that if you affect one life, it is as if you affected the entire world.

As the old man walked the beach at dawn, he noticed a young man ahead of him picking up starfish and flinging them into the sea. Finally catching up with the youth, he asked him why he was doing this. The answer was that the stranded starfish would die if left until the morning sun. "But the beach goes on for miles and there are millions of starfish," countered the other. "How can your effort make any difference?" The young man looked at the starfish in his hand and then threw it to safety in the waves. "It makes a difference to this one."

The Tallit on Kol Nidre
Steve Schwartz

The Kol Nidre service that we have gathered together for this evening is unique in the Jewish calendar for three reasons. The first is the most obvious, the presence of the Kol Nidre prayer itself ~ recited only once a year, at this service. We ask in it that vows we made that we were not able to fulfill during the course of the year that has gone by, be forgiven. The second reason tonight's service is unique is because of the extended prayers we offer after the silent עֲמִידָה (*amidah*) ~ we begin our recitation of the list of sins, we recall before God His qualities of mercy and forgiveness when we sing together the 13 attributes ~ and this is the only evening service of the year where these extra prayers are inserted into the liturgy.

But the third unique Kol Nidre ritual is a little bit different, because it comes not from something that we *say*, but instead from something that we *do*. There is something we do Kol Nidre night that we don't do any other night of the year. Kol Nidre is the only night of the entire year when our tradition asks us to wear a tallit, a prayer shawl.

I love the mitzvah of wearing a tallit, because it is a powerful symbol of the presence of God. In the tradition, we talk about being תַּחַת כַּנְפֵי הַשְּׁכִינָה (*tahat kanfei hashekhina*) ~ under the wings of God ~ and it is in the presence of God, the שְׁכִינָה (*Shekhinah*), that we wrap ourselves through the tallit.

But tallit is also the central symbol of covenant between God and Israel ~ because if you count the fringes, and the wraps, and the loops, you somehow arrive at the number 613 ~ exactly the number of the mitzvot, commandments, that bind us as Jews to God. And, don't forget, the tallit is mentioned in the third paragraph of the Sh'ma, meaning that Jews have been wearing tallitot for at least 3000 years. And that in and of itself is astonishing.

Even so, the tallit, all the rest of the year, is only worn during the day ~ never at night ~ so why tonight on Kol Nidre?

One idea is that the quality of holiness of Yom Kippur is so intensely elevated, that the entire 25-hour period is filled with nonstop prayer, from the moment we begin to fast until the moment our fast is broken. And indeed, not so long ago, the custom on Kol Nidre night was for people to stay all night long in the shul and pray throughout the evening. So the tallit was put on before the Kol Nidre service because you would still be praying when the sun was coming up, which *was* the time to put on a tallit.

But another possibility comes from the midrash (*Pirkei d'Rabi Eliezer,* chapter 46), which believes that the power of Yom Kippur allows us as Jews to enter a higher spiritual plane, and to almost become like the angels themselves. So, says the midrash, just as angels stand in prayer before God, we stand in prayer throughout the 25 hours of Yom Kippur. Just as angels have no need for food or drink, because they are sustained by the spirit of God alone, so we Jews, on Yom Kippur, need not eat or drink. (And just as the angels are united in peace, as Jews on Yom Kippur we come to synagogue and strive to make peace with others and with ourselves). And, finally, just as the tradition imagines that angels are clothed in a shimmering white cloth (Daniel 10:5), so we Jews wear our white kittels ~ white robes, and our white prayer shawls, beginning on this holy night.

Sacred Objects

I have always believed that our ritual objects take on their own symbolic meaning and holiness in our lives ~ and I can't tell you how many times I have had a conversation with someone and they are telling me about some Shabbos candlesticks, or a kiddush cup, or some wedding rings, or an old set of tefillin, or an old tallit, and their eyes just fill up with tears as they talk about these ritual objects. Those things would be worth nothing if we were to take them to a pawn shop, but they are worth everything to us ~ because they become sacred symbols of people we love, of holy moments in our lives, and of the thousands of years of connection between God and Israel that we celebrate.

And so tonight I would like to take a few minutes and tell you about the three tallises I own, about why they are sacred to me. And I would also like to tell you about how these tallises remind me of who I was, how they help me to understand who I am now, and how they give me insight into who I would like to be one day.

The Tallitot: Present, Past, and Future...

The Past...
Do you remember the first tallit you ever wore? It was probably at your Bar Mitzvah, or for a younger generation of women, your Bat Mitzvah. It was probably given to you by people who were very important in your life ~ maybe your bubbe and zayde, maybe your own parents, or a favorite uncle or aunt. When you first got that tallit, you were reminded of your identity as a Jew and also of the new responsibilities that you would have as you reached

the age of religious adulthood. You were proud to wear it, and when you put it over your shoulders, you felt more grown up than you had the day before.

This tallit is the tallit I wore at my bar mitzvah ~ it is worn and fading, the creases in it are deep, like wrinkles we acquire during life, and will never come out. I still wear it on some mornings, and it's funny how when I wore it as boy, I felt more grown up, but when I wear it now as a grown man, I feel younger, because it reminds me of the 13 year-old I used to be and that I still have locked up inside of me.

There is something very beautiful about who we are as children ~ there is an innocence that we had, a wonder at the world, an uncomplicated faith in God, and a sense of security and hope and possibility that is hard to retain as we get older. Do you remember when you were young? How you thought, who you were, what you loved? What you thought you could do and who you thought you could be? Those are things that we lose track of over time, but that we should try to recall on this sacred day.

As it reminds me of my childhood, this tallit also reminds me of my history and the history of my family ~ it was given to me by my bubbe and zayde, and whenever I see it, whenever I wear it, I am reminded of them and of what they gave me in my life. My zayde was a gentle and loving man, who was soft-spoken and intelligent, and who probably never said an unkind word about another person ~ and I thank God that some of that impulse is inside of me. My bubbe was a strong-willed woman who had a deep faith in God and an intense connection to her Judaism, and an unparalleled passion for the importance of family. She lived a long life ~ 99 years ~ and when she died, she had 19 great-grandchildren.

I often will say to a couple that stands under the huppah that they have not arrived at that moment on their own. There are many people who have helped them to reach that sacred moment of their lives, and in a way all of those people share that moment under the huppah. Parents have raised them, loved them, sacrificed for them. Grandparents have given them wisdom, love, and a first-hand connection to the past and their traditions that they would never have otherwise. In so many ways, we truly stand on the shoulders of those who have gone before us, and we walk on the paths that they have paved. The gifts they have given us cannot be measured; at best we can hope to have a sense of what they have done, to be humble when we think about them, and to be thankful for their presence in our lives. On the holidays, and especially, I think, Rosh Hashana, Yom Kippur, and Pesah, we most strongly feel both the presence and the absence of people that we've loved and lost. We feel their absence because we revisit the pain of loss when we say the yizkor prayers, but we feel their presence because we realize on these days how much they gave us during their lives, and how much they still give us every single day.

It is partially that past that we come to shul on Yom Kippur to remember and to honor.

The Present...

But as we come to shul on Yom Kippur to remember our past, we also come here to reflect on our present ~ and the question we are supposed to ask is very simple, but the answer is difficult. The question is, how are we doing right now? Do you remember Ed Koch, the mayor of New York back in the late 70s and early 80s? He had a series of pet phrases he was known for, and one of them was "how am I doing?" When he would walk around, shaking people's hands, this is what he would say to them: how am I doing?

Notice that he didn't ask "how did I do?" in the past tense. He asked how am I doing right now, how are my actions today impacting the people around me, impacting the world around me? And that is a Yom Kippur question. In Ed Koch terms, how are we doing?

That is a present-tense question, and here is my present-tense tallit. It is the tallit I wear every morning when I pray. Like the present, like everyday life, it is colorful, a bit hard to control, it is large, and feels a bit overwhelming sometimes, and it is complicated. But every day when I put it on, it is a reminder to me of the responsibilities that I have as a human being and a Jew; not once a year, or once a week, but every single day. Because when I put it on, I pray and I say things like וְאָהַבְתָּ לְרֵעֲךָ כָּמוֹךָ (*v'ahavta le reiakha kamokha*) ~ that I should love my neighbor as I love myself ~ and everyday, that day, I should remember that means every person I come into contact with. Or I say מִי כָמֹכָה בָּאֵלִים יְיָ (*mi khamokha baeilim Adonai*) ~ that every day I need to consider that it is just by the grace of God that I walk on this earth, and as a Jew I have a responsibility to struggle with relationship with God in my life. Or I say עֹשֶׂה שָׁלוֹם (*oseh shalom*) ~ make peace, God, in this world ~ so that I can remember that peace will only come from human actions, and each one of us must be a part of that process.

But this tallit also reminds me of something closer to home, the responsibility I have to be a good husband and a good father, because this tallit was a gift that Becky gave to me before we were married. And so every day it reminds me of the blessing of family I have in my life, and that I should not take that blessing for granted. Because if my friends think I'm the greatest guy in the world, or if you all think I'm a wonderful rabbi, it doesn't mean anything unless first and foremost I'm a good husband and father.

The Future...

The last tallit I have to tell you about is the one I am wearing right now. I wear it only a few days a year: the days between Rosh Hashana and Yom Kippur, and on the holiday of Yom Kippur itself. This tallit is special to me because the dean of the rabbinical school, on the day of my graduation, gently placed it onto my shoulders ~ and at that moment, I became a rabbi. This tallit represents for me the future, and hope, and possibility. It says something to me about who I would like to be. Except for the blue collar, it is all white, so it is a symbol of purity, and it is purity of soul and spirit that we strive to find on Yom Kippur. And yet, just like our souls, because this tallit is so white, it can be so easily stained. The smallest specs of dirt will show on it, and as time goes by, I know that some dirt will find its way to its surface. But also like our souls, it can be cleaned, and made ~ not new again, but pure again.

The 17th century Danish theologian Soren Kierkegaard wrote that "life must be lived forward, but can only be understood backward." But part of Yom Kippur is designed to make us think about the temporal quality of life, to drive home inside of us the idea that we only have a limited amount of time, and that means that every moment we do have is infinitely precious. Yom Kippur offers us a once-a-year opportunity to have an end-of-life perspective on the meaning of the life we live every day. It is a rare opportunity, and I believe a precious gift from God. And in some ways we could say that Yom Kippur is a day when all of our tallises meet ~ when our past, and our present, and our future come together to give us a perspective on our lives, and to give us an understanding of who we are now and who we might like to be by next Yom Kippur.

Conclusion

One day, please God many years from now, I know that my own time on this earth will come to an end. On that day my children, and if I am very blessed, my grandchildren, will gently lay me down for my final rest. There are many things I don't know about that day. I don't know when it will be, and I don't know what it will be like. But one thing I know is that I will be laid to rest in a tallit, and I know that it is *this* tallit that I will be wearing.

It is a tradition for men to be buried in a tallit they wore during their lives. But when a tallit is used for burial, something has to be done to it to signify that it will no longer be used in this world. And so one of the fringes is cut and removed. So we are always buried in a tallit that is imperfect.

Contained in that old practice are two very beautiful ideas. First, it symbolizes that one of the things that defines us as humans is that we are flawed, we are imperfect. Our greatest efforts, our highest aspirations, our best talents, our hopes and dreams, with God's help produce a wonderful life, a good life, a meaningful life, but you know what? ~ never ever, not even for the greatest of us, never ever a perfect life. That is why we need Kol Nidre not just once, but every year, because every year we will have made mistakes.

Second, the imperfect tallit reminds us that even with our flaws, God will accept our return. And with our flaws, God will take us back, one day, at the end of our lives. But in the same way, with all our flaws, God will take us back every year when we stand before Him with a sincere heart on this holy night of Kol Nidre.

May it be so this year and every year....

From Our Own Clothing to God's Throne:
The True Meaning of the Tallit
Peretz Rodman

The second-century sage Rabbi Meir offered a multi-staged observation on the meaning of the color תְּכֵלֶת (*tekhelet*), a slightly purplish blue dye made ~ so the Talmud tells us ~ from the internal juices (the "blood") of a certain sea creature.

Rabbi Meir is quoted in eight different sources (with slight changes) as having remarked,

> *Tekhelet resembles the sea, and the sea resembles the sky, and the sky resembles the Throne of Glory [on which Adonai is seated], as it is written: 'Above the expanse of their heads was the semblance of a throne, in appearance like sapphire.'*
>
> (Ezekiel 1:26)

What, we may ask, prompted Rabbi Meir's comment? His daisy-chained series of comparisons leads us step-by-step to an answer, but what is the question?

In order to solve this puzzle, we need to consider how and when the individual Jew encountered תְּכֵלֶת (*tekhelet*), in his or her daily life. Tekhelet was one of the colors of a number of Temple appurtenances and some of the High Priest's garments. The High Priest's headdress had a single cord of tekhelet-dyed wool featured prominently in front. But the Temple service figured in the experience of very few people, except on the pilgrim festivals. Even then, only a minority of the residents of the outlying districts made the journey on any given occasion. When they did, their view of the Temple was that of the common folk who were restricted to the outermost precincts.

Tekhelet in Daily Experience

There was, however, תְּכֵלֶת (*tekhelet*) to be glimpsed in one's daily life, and not even from afar. That expensive color was reserved in other ancient Mediterranean societies for royals and nobles, but in the daily routine of every Jew there was occasion to wear a tiny bit of the royal blue. The source of that practice is in a passage from chapter 15 of the Book of Numbers, a passage familiar to anyone acquainted with the traditional Jewish liturgy:

> *Adonai spoke to Moses, saying: 'Speak to the children of Israel, saying to them: they shall make tzitzit/fringes on the wing-corners of their garments throughout their generations, and they shall place on the fringe of the wing-corner a cord of tekhelet. And it shall be for you for a fringe, and you shall see it and recall all the precepts of Adonai and perform them. You are not to go astray after your heart and*

after your eyes, after which you go whoring. I am
Adonai your God, who brought you out of Egypt to
be your God; I, Adonai, am your God.

A careful look at the number and gender of the
Hebrew nouns and pronouns in this passage confirms
what the reader might glean from the translation ~ or
might miss: that the "it" that is to be the visual
reminder of all other mitzvot is not the "fringe"
(צִיצָת - *tzitzit*) but the blue cord פְּתִיל תְּכֵלֶת (*petil*
tekhelet) that it contains.

A World Devoid of Tekhelet

That the פְּתִיל תְּכֵלֶת (*petil tekhelet*) is the core of this
mitzvah is not immediately evident to those familiar
with how Jewish law has come to deal with the
details of this requirement and with its interpretation.
The tradition of wearing the פְּתִיל תְּכֵלֶת (*petil tekhelet*)
was undermined very early by the scarcity of the dye,
so much so that the Mishnah, at the end of the second
century CE, includes a dispensation for one who
cannot gain access to wool dyed with tekhelet to wear
צִיצָת (*tzitzit*) entirely of undyed wool. [Somewhat
outlandishly, it offers us the opposite option as well:
should we somehow find ourselves with a surfeit of
wool dyed with tekhelet but no access to undyed
wool, we may make our צִיצָת (*tzitzit*) entirely of the
staggeringly expensive threads.]

Apparently, the Mishnah is informing us that the part of the biblical verse that enjoins us to place צִיצָת (*tzitzit*) on our four-cornered garments remains in force even when we cannot fulfill the continuation of the verse by including a strand of תְּכֵלֶת (*tekhelet*). These are two separate and independent requirements. And in fact, once the תְּכֵלֶת (*tekhelet*) industry died out (due in part to competition from cheap vegetable dyes) and the manufacturing process was lost around the ninth century CE, Jews used only undyed wool in their צִיצָת (*tzitzit*).

In this milieu, a variety of traditions sprang up in which the meaning of צִיצָת (*tzitzit*) is displayed in the numbers of twists and knots in the strands that form the fringe at each corner of the tallit, the four-cornered garment that is the vehicle for the צִיצָת (*tzitzit*). In each of these traditions, God's holy Name or the declaration "Sh'ma Yisrael" is somehow encoded in the numbers of those twists and knots. That would seem to provide an answer to an exegetical question raised by the sequence of thoughts in the passage from Numbers 15. What is the logic of "you shall see it and recall all the precepts of Adonai and perform them?" How is it that viewing the צִיצָת (*tzitzit*) stimulates thoughts of the divine commandments? The numerology of the צִיצָת (*tzitzit*) strands provides an answer.

Tekhelet: Essential Indeed?

If the fundamental code of rabbinic law, the Mishnah, understands צִיצָת (*tzitzit*) to be a separate mitzvah, independent of the תְּכֵלֶת (*tekhelet*) strand, on what basis can we claim that our reading of the Torah's law, which posits that the essence of the entire mitzvah is the blue cord, is correct and authoritative? Several clues in rabbinic literature support our contention. We will offer only one of those clues here.

The story of Korah, the leader of the rebellion against the authority of Moses in the Book of Numbers, follows immediately upon the passage about צִיצָת (*tzitzit*) cited above. This juxtaposition led to the invention of a rabbinic legend in which Korah ~ in some versions at the insistence of his crafty and ambitious wife ~ posed questions to Moses that cast doubt on the sense, and thus the veracity, of the Torah's laws, which were then being promulgated by Moses in the name of God. The first of those challenges was this: "A tallit made entirely of [wool dyed with] תְּכֵלֶת (*tekhelet*) ~ is it still liable for the mitzvah of צִיצָת (*tzitzit*)?"

The Torah's laws relate, of course, to the normal range of circumstances. Such an exquisite garment as a tallit made entirely of tekhelet-dyed wool was unattainably expensive, a purely fanciful invention. Garments of four (or more) corners are required to have צִיצָת (*tzitzit*), and every Israelite is enjoined to go to the expense of adding a single contrasting strand of tekhelet to each corner. To anyone who insists on asking, "Even if the garment is all tekhelet?" the answer is, in fact, "Yes, even then." Despite the apparent lack of logic in requiring the minor appendage when the entire garment pronounces to all its message of nobility and sanctity, a law is still a law, and in theory would have to be applied even in that wildly unlikely case.

Korah's intent aside, we can deduce from his cunning question that the blue cord was thought to be the essential fact of the צִיצָת (*tzitzit*). If not, what would be the logic of the suggestion that perhaps an all-tekhelet garment would be exempt from the entire mitzvah of צִיצָת (*tzitzit*)? The question, after all, was not whether the צִיצָת (*tzitzit*) would still need a blue cord but whether צִיצָת (*tzitzit*) would be required at all, thus supporting the contention that in some circles, at least, and despite the Mishnah's dispensation, wearing צִיצָת (*tzitzit*) without פְּתִיל תְּכֵלֶת (*petil tekhelet*) was considered to be an incomplete fulfillment of what was viewed as one integrated mitzvah.

Petil Tekhelet as an Object of Meditation
Now we can appreciate the task Rabbi Meir set for himself and fully comprehend his solution. Given that what we are to look at is the blue cord, what is the logic of the vision-memory-performance nexus?

Rabbi Meir provides us with an answer. The blue of the cord in our צִיצָת (*tzitzit*) should serve to remind us of all the iridescent blue we see when our vision encompasses whole realms of Creation: the transparent water of the sea that appears blue before our eyes, the transparent air of the skies that reveals itself in that same hue, and on from Creation to Creator: the invisible God whose throne, the edge of which is the pinnacle of what can be seen by the prophets, appears in that very same purple-tinged blue.

What better association, what better object of meditation, could there be than the ancient royal blue for a nation that aspires to be "a kingdom of priests and a holy nation"? Once again we rely on the comments of Rabbi Meir, in whose opinion "anyone who fulfills the mitzvah of צִיצָת (*tzitzit*) is regarded by Scripture as if he had welcomed the שְׁכִינָה (*Shekhinah*) ~ the Divine Presence."

Lehitatef Batzitzit:
Recovering the Meaning of the Tallit
Kenneth R. Leitner

I first noticed it about a year and a half ago, when we moved into our newly built synagogue and began our Shabbat morning minyan, but I paid it no mind. An elder of the congregation would don his tallit (prayer shawl) by simply lifting it over his shoulders. All of the other congregants went through some ritual motions ~ blessing, kissing, wrapping. Later in the service, at the recitation of the Sh'ma, when we gather the צִיצָת - *tzitzit* (tassels) and kiss them, the pattern was repeated: all of the other congregants went through all or at least some of the ritual motions. This one congregant, my elder, sat on the sidelines doing none of the ritual.

I know the man well ~ a pillar of the community, a leader of the Jewish retirement community in our area, a faithful attendee of services in our synagogue or at the retirement center, a former chairman of the

Bonds for Israel and the UJA, a trustee of the congregation during our building program. His labeling of much of our ritual as nostalgia for tradition is a function of his extremely liberal religious background. Were he to engage in the ritual motions, it would be an affectation.

For others, too, such ritual motions are affectations. Some congregants engage only partially in the motions in order to avoid that which is not natural to them. For some, it is the act of doing, the physical motion, that is the barrier. For many, this physical barrier would be overcome if the symbolism and meaning inherent in the rituals were known ~ not only those traditional meanings and symbols that have been crystallized into the prayer book, but also new meanings and associations.

We find in the Torah the commandment to make צִיצַת (*tzitzit*) on the corners of our garments and to include in the tassels a thread of blue (Num. 15:38-41). We are supposed to look upon the צִיצַת (*tzitzit*) and the thread of blue in order to remember and perform all of God's commandments, and not to follow our own base impulses and desires. This remembering and doing is the means by which we become sanctified קְדֹשִׁים (*kedoshim*).

The mitzvah of צִיצַת (*tzitzit*) is elaborated widely in post-biblical Jewish literature. Many meanings and associations are developed that are carried forward in the traditional liturgy, as well as in the widely used texts with commentaries that are found in the synagogue. In our day, the focus is on wearing the tallit with צִיצָת (*tzitzit*) during prayer, and on the associations connected with the rituals of donning and wearing the tallit. In the traditional liturgy, we are directed to two meditative texts prior to donning the tallit.[1] The first is taken from Psalm 104:

> *Bless Adonai, O my soul*
> *Adonai, my God, You are very great*
> *You are clothed in glory and majesty*
> *Enveloped in light as a garment*
> *Spreading the heavens as a vast curtain.*

The very strong visual imagery gives meaning to our anticipation of the physical action of wrapping the tallit around the body and head completely. We anticipate becoming surrounded by the Glory and Majesty of God, and being enveloped by God's light. We anticipate the drawing back of the tallit from our eyes as the heavenly curtain is drawn back so that we can see the unfolding of creation.

The second meditation is rooted in kabbalah, and often begins with a statement about the unification of God's name:

> For the sake of unifying the Blessed Holy One
> and the divine Presence...with reverence and
> love...for the sake of unifying the ה-י (*Yod-Heh*)
> with the ה-ו (*Vav-Heh*) into a complete unity...
> And in the name of all Israel....

As I enwrap my body in the צִיצִת (*tzitzit*), so
may my soul and my 248 limbs and my 365
sinews be enwrapped in the light of the צִיצִת
(*tzitzit*), totaling 613. Just as I am covered with
a tallit in this world, so may I merit the mantle
of learning and a beautiful tallit in the world to
come, in Gan Eden.

By means of the mitzvah of צִיצִת (*tzitzit*), may
my soul, my spirit, my essence be guarded from
obstructions. May the tallit spread its wings
over them and save them "like an eagle who
rouses his nestlings, hovering over his young"
(Deut. 32:11). And may the performance of this
mitzvah of צִיצִת (*tzitzit*) before the Blessed
Holy One be accounted as if I have fulfilled all
613 mitzvot in all parts, details, and intentions.
Amen. Selah.[2]

Visual Imagery

Here too the visual imagery is suggestive and
focusing. The entire physical and spiritual self is to be
wrapped in the light of the צִיצִת (*tzitzit*), God's light.
The tallit is suggestive of the messianic future. It is at
once illuminating and also sheltering and protective.

This meditation complete, we proceed physically to
enwrap ourselves in the tallit. While wrapped, with
the tallit around the head and shoulders, another
meditation is recited that is also taken from the
Psalms (36:8-11):

How precious is your faithful care, 0 God!
Humankind shelters in the shadow of Your wings.
They feast on the rich fare of Your house;
You let them drink at Your refreshing stream.
With You is the fountain of life;
by Your light do we see light.
Bestow Your faithful care on those devoted to You,
and Your beneficence on upright people.

The conjoining of these meditations with the physical is designed to produce a "peak experience." If only for an instant, light envelops us through a tallit that is suggestive of a divine radiance before we draw back the tallit to begin our prayers.

The imagery is powerful, and given the mystical origin or potential for interpretation in the meditations, it may be mystically engaging. Yet its effect can only be experienced when the fullness of the ritual in both word and action is engaged. Most Jews are unfamiliar with the texts or with the ideas they contain, and they are uncomfortable with the suggestive mystical tone of the meditations. These factors combine to reduce the peak experience to a mundane action for the overwhelming majority of worshipers. For some, the study of the ritual in both word and action will allow them entry into an enriched awareness and appreciation of the symbolism involved. For most worshipers, however, it will neither engage nor stimulate.

Discomfort with Mysticism

The same discomfort and reaction to the mystical has resulted in the editing out of some or all of the meditation in many contemporary liturgies. The worshiper is thus left with little or no symbolism to encounter. When the third paragraph of the Sh'ma is skipped over in the service, there is then no engagement with both the ritual motions and ideas connected with the צִיצָת (*tzitzit*).

It is in the third paragraph of the Sh'ma that we are called upon once again to engage in a prescribed ritual motion with the צִיצָת (*tzitzit*). Traditionally, we draw together the four corners of the tallit with the צִיצָת (*tzitzit*) immediately before the Sh'ma, at the phrase "Bring us in peace from the four corners of the earth." We hold the צִיצָת (*tzitzit*) during the recitation of the Sh'ma, and some will cover the eyes with the hand in an act of unification. During the recitation of the third paragraph, we kiss the צִיצָת (*tzitzit*) each time the term is mentioned, an expression of reverence and affection for God and Torah. The section of the Torah recited (Num. 15:37-41) is less suggestive of mystical ideas than the Psalms texts found in the meditations. The difficulty here rests with the physical action that is required and the lack of meaning associated with this action, or the abstractness of the notion of showing affection for God and Torah.

New Interpretations

It is possible to re-engage people by drawing new meanings and teaching new interpretations that are stimulating, emotionally satisfying, and intellectually honest. Many such meanings flow from the physical motions if we disconnect these motions from their accumulated interpretations.

The physical motions associated with donning the tallit are suggestive of an interpretation that stands in tension with the ideas crystallized in the prayer book. Visualizing the act of wrapping the tallit around body and head, we become aware of an extreme sense of isolation. This sense of aloneness is acute if we stand in the freezing winter of distant, barren Russia, far into the exile of every prisoner of conscience. Pulling the tallit tightly around, the bars of black pass before our eyes like the jailer's door. We can release the tallit and easily escape our imprisonment. They cannot now and will not ever be able to escape unless we are willing to act on their behalf.

Twice in the third paragraph of the Sh'ma we are told to remember. We may ask midrashically why it is necessary to include two references to remembering. Surely the added reference is intended as a prod to greater awareness of and sense of responsibility to all Jews everywhere. This idea of remembering strikes deeply elsewhere. *Zakhor*, remember. As the dark bars flash in front of the eyes in contrast to the light background, we can see dark ink, numbers, on the light background of pale flesh.

The adornment of the tallit with a variety of colors suggests a different experience. We can stand with Noah as the full range of color is arrayed before our eyes as a rainbow. With all humankind, we become participants in the covenant between God and the earth. For a brief moment, we stand enveloped by the rainbow, and as it is drawn away, we are returned to our fragile life on earth. Our responsibilities to this covenant can thus be renewed daily. A similar sensation can be experienced by those whose tallit is of a simple design. As the stripes of a single color pass before our eyes, we can experience an incomplete rainbow, a rainbow in potential, on which we must build.

Yet a different interpretation emerges from the ritual motions that accompany the recitation of the Sh'ma. The act of kissing the צִיצָת (*tzitzit*) as an expression of reverence and affection for God and Torah is deeply grounded in custom. For many, this is an unfortunate affectation, but a powerful interpretation can invest the act with purpose.

Just such an interpretation flows from the juxtaposition of the phrase "Bring us together" and the kissing of the צִיצָת (*tzitzit*). We focus on the us in the beginning of the phrase. This us is the people

Israel ~ all of us. Through the צִיצָת (*tzitzit*), we are able to express our affection for all Jews everywhere.

The צִיצָת (*tzitzit*) therefore come to represent an ideal of which we need to be conscious every day. This interpretation merges well with the idea that enwrapping can lead to a sense of identification with the Jews in forced exile. For a brief moment, we share their solitude and pain. We then embrace them and show our love for them with a symbolic kiss.

Another interpretation emerges from this focus on us and the symbolic use of the צִיצָת (*tzitzit*) as the people Israel. We have focused primarily on the ritual motions of wrapping the tallit as a means of identifying with our brothers and sisters in exile. We are able to share for a moment their exile and pain. Aloneness and isolation are real Jewish issues. Not only for the Jew in exile, but for any Jew who is by circumstance isolated from the community. We can take the tallit and wrap it around ourselves, no matter where we are, and feel enfolded in and embraced by our people. These few interpretations are examples of the way in which a Jewish ritual can be revitalized if the traditional meanings of the rituals do not engage or stimulate the worshiper. Used as part of a teaching program or as a stimulus to new literary creativity that will be of liturgical worth, these interpretations reach out and address all contemporary Jews.

---

[1]My purposes here are interpretive and not scholarly, and for these interpretive purposes, a broad latitude is taken that intertwines tallit and tzitzit. For an important scholarly essay that draws on a wide range of the classical and interpretive literature, see Ben-Zion Bokser, "The Thread of Blue," in *The Proceedings of the American Academy for Jewish Research* 31(1963): 1-32.

[2] This meditation is freely translated from the text in the *Siddur Olat Re'iyah* of Rabbi Abraham Isaac Kook. Rabbi Kook's lengthy commentary is an outstanding example of the mystical interpretation of the tzitzit. On the opening phrase: "For the sake of unifying," see chapter XII ("The Polemic on the Recital of le-Shem Yihud") of Louis Jacobs, *Hasidic Prayer* (New York: Schocken, 1973).

The Tallit and its Symbolism
Martin Samuel Cohen

The tallit ~ the prayer shawl ~ is not a ritual item *per se*. Therefore, it is an odd item to have become so well-known and ubiquitous a symbol of Judaism and Jewish life. At first appraisal it seems to be a garment designed to hold up the tzitzit ~ fringes ~ attached to it, but if that is its sole purpose, the tallit must certainly be the most elaborate "holder" of a ritual object in Jewish practice. Moreover, there is the unique aspect of self-necessitation to consider: one wears a tallit because of its tzitzit, but one is required to wear tzitzit only because one is wearing a tallit in the first place! Since the obligation to wear ritual fringes devolves only upon one wearing four-cornered garments, one could theoretically be free of the obligation merely by removing the four-cornered garment.[1]

The tallit, therefore, must do more than merely hold up its fringes. Generally speaking, we perform the commandments as they become incumbent, not when we can somehow create an artificial situation requiring their observance. If we put on the tallit only in order to obligate ourselves to perform the mitzvah of wearing tzitzit, it would be quite anomalous and would require an explanation of some sort. At least as plausible is the possibility that the fringes are of lesser importance, and that they are attached to the tallit simply because it is a four-cornered garment which may not be worn without fringes. This would allow us to focus on the tallit itself and try to explain its use as a ritual garment independent of the fringes which hang from its corners.

When the noted psychoanalyst Theodor Reik suggested that the tallit is really a wool covering intended to complement the leather straps of the tefillin, as a quasi-shamanistic (if subconscious) attempt on the part of the Jew to dress up like his ancient totem animal, he was right and wrong.[2] He was wrong, because the idea that Israel once worshiped its God through the totemistic symbol of a sacred beast is untenable, unproven and highly unlikely. But Reik was right, in that he correctly perceived that the wearing of the tallit is an act of *imitatio Dei*, in terms of both its mythological and symbolic foundations.

When wrapping oneself in a tallit one recites the psalmist's declaration, "In Your light we shall see light,"[3] which unavoidably recalls to us the description of God elsewhere in the Psalms as one who "wears light as a garment."[4] The second verse sheds its own light on the first and explains the point of its liturgical usage: one wraps oneself in the tallit to imitate the God of Israel bathed in primal light, the stuff of Creation.[5] The task then is to explain why one would do such a thing. In other words, we must explain the symbolism that makes the act meaningful and why, of all divine acts, this wrapping in a garment of light is worthy of such prominent ritual imitation.

To begin to deal with these questions, we must first appreciate the meaning of clothing to the ancients.

Clothing in Ancient Traditions

At the first level of symbolic thought, we find the garment standing in for the person who wears it. For a potent example, we may turn to the Biblical cycle of Joseph stories. The initial identification of Joseph and his garment is in the first Joseph story to be presented in Genesis ~ the story of his brothers' enmity toward him and his subsequent sale by them into Egypt.[6] Recall that it was the garment Jacob had given to Joseph that set his brothers against him in the first place. When Jacob mourns the death of Joseph (whom he assumes, incorrectly, to have been killed), the body is missing and Jacob is left to mourn over the empty garment that symbolizes Joseph both to him and to us. When Jacob cries out, "Joseph is surely ripped apart!" (Genesis 37:33), it is not Joseph's torn body but his torn coat that he is clasping. "And Jacob ripped his (own) clothing..." (Genesis 37:34). This universal act of mourning symbolizes the destruction of self towards which the mourner is inclined but which society forbids him. Here, Jacob's act of ripping his clothing is particularly poignant. He holds the garment that symbolizes his mangled son and responds without indulging his grief in mixed metaphor: he mangles himself in response by ripping his own clothing.

Joseph later acquires a new garment, which plays its own role in the events of the last quarter of Genesis. Only by grabbing Joseph's garment as he flees is the wife of Potiphar able to convince her husband that it was Joseph who had tried to seduce her, not the reverse. "And she grabbed him by his garment, saying, 'Sleep with me!' but he fled, leaving the garment in her hand, and he went outside" (Genesis 39:12). Again, the garment is assimilated to the wearer and Potiphar has no trouble identifying the garment. "And Joseph's master took him and put him in prison" (Genesis 39:20).

An ancient exegete understood that the counterpart to this story is the subsequent reference to Joseph's corpse: "And Moses took Joseph's bones with him" (Exodus 13:19) in accordance with Joseph's wishes. Joseph had lived in both Palestine and Egypt, represented in Palestine by his torn coat after his descent into Egypt. In death he was also represented in both places ~ in Egypt after the Exodus (and the concurrent removal of his bones) by the cloak he left behind in his first master's house. This might account for the fact that the usually succinct pentateuchal text refers to the garment five separate times within seven verses.[7]

In a midrash attributed to an otherwise unknown Simon of Kitron, we learn:

> *Because of the merit accrued by Joseph's bones*
> *[being present at the Red Sea], the Sea was split.*
> *[This we learn by virtue of the fact that] the verb*
> *"to flee" is used both of the sea, in "The sea saw and*
> *fled" (Psalms 114:3), and of Joseph, in "He fled... and*
> *he went outside" (Genesis 39:12).*[8]

This version intimates that the link between the abandoned garment and the retrieved bones was metaphorically applied to two related situations, so that the flight of Joseph from his master's wife brought about the flight of the sea, and the ripped garment prefigured and predicted the ripped sea through which Israel fled.[9]

The basic idea, though, is that the garment represents the wearer. Joseph's garments allowed him to exist in two places at the same time, at least on the level of midrashic reality. From this point it is easy to understand how the basic idea was elaborated, on a less midrashic and more metaphysical plane: the wearer and the garment worn become symbolic of the two aspects of any human being ~ the physical body and the soul it harbors.

This is the plane of symbolic thought on which the ritual use of the tallit seems to rest. The basic idea can be developed in either of two ways. Either the soul is seen as a kind of garment which the physical body of an individual wears or else, in a slightly more complicated configuration, the body encased in its garment (so to speak) is itself seen as symbolic of the soul encased by the physical body it inhabits.

Depending on the specifics of the symbolic construct, then, both the act of putting the garment on and the act of taking it off can bear interpretation as representing personal redemption.

In the Syriac *Hymn of the Pearl*, one of the most appealing of all gnostic tales, we read of a young prince whose parents take away his robe of glory and send him back to Egypt to bring back the one pearl that "lies in the middle of the sea, which is enriched by the snorting serpent." He puts on Egyptian garments when he arrives, but he overeats, becomes drunk and forgets the pearl. Finally a letter comes for the prince from his parents:

> *From thy father, the King of kings, and from thy*
> *mother, mistress of the East, and from thy brother,*
> *our next in rank, greeting. Awake and rise up out*

of thy sleep and perceive the words of our letter.
Remember that thou art a king's son: behold whom
thou hast served in bondage. Be mindful of the Pearl,
for whose sake thou hast departed into Egypt.
Remember thy robe of glory, recall thy splendid
mantle, that thou mayest put them on and deck
thyself with them and thy name be read in the book
of the heroes and thou become with thy brother, heir
in our kingdom.[10]

The letter has the desired effect upon the prince; he recalls his mission, seizes the pearl, and returns home. Upon his return home, he puts on his garment and describes the experience in the following remarkable language which I can do no better than to offer in A. A. Bevan's translation:

And my bright robe, which I had stripped off,
And the toga wherewith it was wrapped,
From the heights of Hyrcania
My parents sent thither,
By the hand of their treasurers
Who in their faithfulness could be trusted therewith.
And because I remembered not its fashion ~
For in my childhood I had left it in my father's house ~
On a sudden, as I faced it,
The garment seemed to me like a mirror of myself.
I saw it all in my whole self;
Moreover, I faced my whole self in (facing) it.
For we were two in distinction
And yet again one in one likeness.
And the treasurers also,
Who brought it to me, I saw in like manner

> *That they were twain (yet) one likeness,*
> *For one kingly sign was graven on them,*
> *Of his hands that restored to me (?)*
> *My treasure and my wealth by means of them,*
> *My bright embroidered robe,*
> *Which ... with glorious colors,*
> *With gold and with beryls,*
> *And rubies and agates (?)*
> *And sardonyxes varied in color,*
> *It was also made ready in its home on high (?).*
> *And with stones of adamant*
> *All its seams were fastened.*
> *And the image of the King of kings*
> *Was depicted in full all over it.*
> *And like the sapphire-stone also*
> *Were its manifold hues.*
> *Again, I saw that all over it*
> *The motions of knowledge were stirring,*
> *And as if to speak*
> *I saw it also making itself ready.*[11]

Let us analyze the image of the robe in this passage. It is clear that the robe is not merely a garment. It represents the archetypal prince, the soul, so to speak, that the prince of necessity left in the realm of light (its only appropriate place) when he descended to the world of matter (here symbolized by Egypt) incarnate (dressed in Egyptian garments) to rescue the pearl. The symbolism behind the pearl is not really obvious, but from the context of the standard gnostic myth (of which this passage is an undeniable poetic adaptation), it would appear that the pearl represents those particles of light from the upper realm that need to be redeemed. As such, they are the celestial counterparts of the human soul, the redemption of which signals the onset of the redemptive stage of the human experience.

> *Whereas almost all other expressions (used to symbolize the soul) can apply equally to divinity unimpaired and to its sunken part, the pearl denotes specifically the latter in the fate that has overtaken it. The pearl is essentially the lost pearl and has to be retrieved.*[12]

Consequently, the garment plays the counterpart to the pearl, for while the latter is the symbol of the soul sunken in the world, requiring redemption and captive to a dragon, the former is the soul's archetype that resides in heaven and longs to be reunited with its earthly counterpart. It is also apparent why the garment has at once the image of the king and the prince on it: it *can* have both images because the soul is made in the divine image, so both images resemble each other. It must have those images because it must be identified for the reader as the prince's alter ego (in a terrestrial sense) and as his soul (in the metaphysical sense).

Perhaps this notion lies behind the image, in the Gospels, of soldiers dividing Jesus' cloak by lots in the shadow of the cross.[13] The author of Luke reports that it was Herod who dressed up Jesus in a fine cloak to make him look more pathetic to Pilate, but Matthew attributes this to Roman soldiers: "Then they stripped him and made him wear a scarlet cloak (to mock his claim to be king of the Jews)... and when they finished making fun of him, they took off his cloak and dressed him in his own clothing and led him away to crucify him."[14] Later, after Jesus was crucified, this garment was divided among the soldiers by lots as trophies of their day's work.[15] The ripping of the garment by the soldiers is intended to prefigure the imminent redemption of Jesus, much as the Rabbis recalled the ripped garment of Joseph at the moment of Israel's redemption. The image of Jesus being dressed in the royal purple as a sign of humiliation, only to be reclad in his own garments at the hour of his redemption, is precisely the story of the prince in the *Hymn of the Pearl*, with an ironical twist: the prince's garments of royalty are symbols of the Self whence he came and to which he must return, but the garments of Jesus (corresponding to the Egyptian garments of the prince) represent the earthy shell necessary to be shed before the ascent to the upper world becomes feasible.

The removal of the garments is therefore symbolic of both the negative result of the separation of body and soul, i.e., death, and the positive result, i.e., redemption. The Jewish act, however, is not the removal of the tallit; it is rather donning it. If the garment represents the soul, then what does donning the garment mean if not the re-souling of the individual worshiper, an idea already presented prominently in the early morning liturgy.[16]

The symbolism, however, is not quite complete. If the donning of the tallit symbolizes the restoration of the soul each morning, then it cannot be viewed as a real act of *imitatio Dei*, which we have suggested ought to be the case. How, then, does the idea develop?

Garment as Symbol

The garment at first symbolizes the earthly aspect of the wearer. This enables it to develop into a metaphoric stand-in for the world. That greatest of all Jewish allegorists, Philo, does not discuss Joseph's robe in this sense in any of his extant works, but he does elaborate upon another robe, the robe of the High Priest.

The High Priest, the living nexus between the divine realm and the mundane realm, fittingly wears a robe that symbolizes the world. Philo elaborates his initial premise that the robe represents the world:

> *The gown is all of violet, and is thus an image of the air, for the air is naturally black and, so to speak, a robe reaching to the feet, since it stretches down from the region below the moon to the ends of the earth, and spreads out everywhere. And therefore the gown, too, spreads out from the breast to the feet around the whole body. At the*

ankles, there stand out from it pomegranates and flower trimming and bells. The earth is represented by the flowers, for all that flowers and grows comes from the earth, the water by the pomegranates or flowing fruit, so aptly called from their flowing juice, while the bells represent the harmonious alliance of these two, since life cannot be produced by earth without water, or by water without the substance of the earth, but only by the union and combination of both. Their position testifies most clearly to this explanation. For, just as the pomegranates, the flowers and the bells are at the extremities of the long robe, so too what these symbolize, namely earth and water, occupy the lowest place in the universe, and in unison with the harmony of the All display their several powers at fixed revolutions of time and at their proper seasons....[17]*

The image of the High Priest wrapped in the world-cloak symbolizes the soul wrapped in the body. It may be compared to the expression which, the Koran records, was twice used by Allah to call his prophet. At the beginning of the Al-Middathir sura, the prophet is called:

O thou shrouded in thy mantle
arise and warn!
Thy Lord magnify, thy robes purify,
and defilement flee![18]

Similarly, at the beginning of the Al-Muzamil sura we find:

O thou enwrapped in thy robes,
keep vigil the night ... behold, we
shall cast upon thee a weighty word.[19]

The prophet indicates that his message is for all men, not for himself alone, by showing how Allah spoke to him as one dressed in a cloak. The cloak here does not come to assure us that the prophet was not naked. Rather, it places him in the same role that Philo reserves for the High Priest ~ the Man in the world who symbolizes the world, and whose own Self stands in the space between the divine and mundane realms and makes of him the living nexus between them.

The figures of the priest and the prophet coincide in Jeremiah, who also uses a garment to symbolize that part of himself that is identical with the collective self of his people:

Thus said God to me: "Go and buy a linen girdle;
put it around your loins and do not wash it out with
water." And so I bought such a girdle, in accord with
the divine command, and I put it on.[20]

The prophet must wear the garment, which is to say that it must become assimilated to his body and person if its symbolic potential is to be realized. It is linen and unwashed, which is to say, stiff and uncomfortable. It is the soul itself, attached to the body by divine fiat despite the fact that it is uncomfortable and scratchy. But the story goes further:

> *And God spoke a second time, saying, "Take the*
> *girdle which you bought and put it on and go*
> *to the Euphrates and hide it there in the rocky*
> *crags." And I went and hid it there, as God had*
> *commanded me. And after many days had passed,*
> *God spoke to me and said, "Get up and go to the*
> *Euphrates and get the girdle which I commanded*
> *to you to hide there." And I went and dug it out*
> *and took it from the place in which I had hidden it,*
> *and behold, it was destroyed and utterly useless.*
> *And God spoke to me, saying, "Thus shall I destroy*
> *the pride of Judah and Jerusalem...."* [21]

The girdle here is a symbol of the people. The prophet must first wear the girdle to effect its identification with the fate of the selves of his people through his own Self, which it symbolizes. Jeremiah makes an interesting foil to the prince whose journey we have discussed. The prince traveled to the West to find his soul intact and able to be reunited with his celestial self. The prophet travels East to find his girdle destroyed and useless. The girdle may be destroyed, but it still exists. It symbolizes, more precisely, the ever existent but disengaged Self. But who, or what, is this higher Self in Jewish tradition? The prophet senses our need to know, and gives us his answer: it is the national Self, functioning here as the very soul of God.

Just as a girdle sticks to a man's loins, so did I
stick with the entire House of Israel and the entire
House of Judah, that they be my people...
but they declined to listen.... [22]

The notion that the people Israel serves as the soul of God is a daring speculative idea that can hardly be taken seriously except perhaps within the rarefied realm of symbolic thought. Yet the very idea that the disintegration of the prophet's girdle is meant to foreshadow the destruction of God's people cannot easily bear alternate interpretation. So we have here, then, an interesting development: the use of the garment to suggest negative redemption, i.e., the destruction of the soul, the people.

God wears a garment. It is woven of the collected souls of the Jewish people and, as such, it entitles the Jewish people to consider itself the people of God. The people represent the divine Soul, just as the girdle represents the prophet's inner soul.

But Jewish tradition knows of another garment in the divine wardrobe. Elsewhere we learn that it was precisely in a garment of primeval light that God swathed Himself at the moment of creation. This tradition is already found in the Bible.

He wears light as a garment;
He stretches out the heavens as a curtain.[23]

The ancient Rabbis seem to have been disturbed that God should dress differently on different occasions, and thus perhaps they understood that God's garment of light must eventually be identified with the Jewish nation in its celestial archetypal form, to preserve the integrity of the poet and the prophet. They declined to make that identification explicit, perhaps because such a discovery would radically alter the national self-conception and would be unwanted and undesired encouragement to the masses to seek to ascend through the heavens to view the divine Self ~ a trip the directions for which were known to some but not to many, and regarding which public instruction was expressly forbidden.[24] Thus the tradition was transmitted privately.

> *Rabbi Simon ben Yehotzedek asked Rabbi Samuel ben Nahmani: "Since you are a master of Jewish lore, tell me, whence was the light [i.e., the primeval light that was created three days before the sun, moon and stars) created?" He replied, "The Holy One, blessed be He, wrapped Himself up in it as in a garment and the splendor of its glory shone throughout the universe." This he said in a whisper. He [Rabbi Simon] said to him, "Why are you whispering? The doctrine is explicitly stated in the Bible" [therefore, there is no particular reason to teach this as though it were an esoteric doctrine]. He replied, "I heard it taught in a whisper [that is, as esoterica] and so do I teach it in a whisper."[25]*

The earliest Jewish mystics who did preserve and speculate on these esoteric traditions understood quite well that the garment contains secrets within its nature that could drive one to distraction, so sublime the knowledge that one would acquire. One text of ancient mystics, *Hekhalot Rabbati*, offers a hymn that describes the divine garment, or rather that describes the experience of gazing upon it:

> *A quality of holiness, a quality of power,*
> *A quality of fearfulness, a quality of sublimity,*
> *A quality of trembling, a quality of shaking,*
> *A quality of terror, a quality of consternation,*
> *Is the quality of the garment of Zohariel, YHVH,*
> *God of Israel,*
> *Who comes crowned to the Throne of His Glory*
> *And it is, every part, engraved within and without*
> *YHVH YHVH*
> *And of no creature are the eyes able to behold it,*
> *Not the eyes of flesh and blood and not the eyes of*
> *His servants,*
> *And as for him who does behold it, or sees or glimpses it,*
> *Whirling gyrations grip the balls of his eyes.*
> *And the balls of his eyes cast out and send forth*
> *torches of fire*
> *And these enkindle him and these burn him.*
> *For the fire which comes out from the man who beholds,*
> *This enkindles him and this burns him....*[26]

The hymn is describing something hidden and obscure, but something which is desirable to know for its own sake. There is no intimation here that the garment is a symbol, nor does the hymn express itself in terms of simile. The garment exists and, as such, provokes speculation. The faithful are almost defined as those who engage in such speculation; setting some of the details in a poetic context for the masses is a kindness and a boon for the public. Thus it is that the garment can function equally effectively in the realm of myth as in the adjacent realms of simile, symbol or metaphor.[27]

A Path through Metaphor and Magic to Jewish Ritual

Certain ideas can function in a variety of metaphoric realms. Thus they are able to appear independent of considerations of time or space in different literary corpora as a sort of *leitmotif*. To show how the idea that donning a garment can pave the way to personal redemption, we might consider a story from an entirely different context that tells, basically, the same story.

Sir Gawain, who pledged for a variety of reasons (upon which his honor and prestige depend) to allow the Green Knight one chop at his neck with an axe, is able to escape with only a light cut because he is protected by a green girdle given to him by the wife of his host the previous night. On the way to the Green Channel to suffer his fate, he had stayed with a host and his lady. Three times she had tried to seduce him, but his code of chivalrous behavior was too strong to allow him to succumb, despite the fact (or perhaps especially because of the fact) that he was to end his life on the next day. She finally succeeds in one small way: she offers him a green girdle, a piece of silk, which will protect him.

> *She gracefully grasped the girdle of her gown*
> *Which went round her waist under the wonderful mantle,*
> *A girdle of green silk with a golden hem*
> *Embroidered only at the edges,*
> *with a hand-stitched ornament,*
> *And she pleaded with the prince in a pleasant manner,*
> *But he told her he could touch no treasure at all,*
> *Not gold or any gift, till God gave him grace*
> *to pursue to success the search he was bound on.*
> *So I entreat you to be contented, therefore,*
> *And press no more....*[28]

When Sir Gawain learns that it is a magic garment that makes man "safe from assailants, whoever strives to slay him," he accepts. Because of the slight impropriety involved in his acceptance of the girdle, it does not rescue him entirely, but he escapes with a slight nick in his skin. After the ordeal, Gawain learns that it is the Green Knight himself in whose castle he had lodged and whose wife had presented him with the magic girdle. He tries to return it, but the Green Knight presses him to keep it as an appropriate trophy.

Who is this Green Knight who extends, via his messenger/wife, a girdle that protects from harm and that he himself symbolizes? The girdle is a piece of silk; it cannot really protect. Rather, it symbolizes that portion of Gawain that cannot be harmed, that needs no protection. The Self is indestructible. The realization of that truth enables Gawain to find a friend rather than an executioner in the Green Knight. In the same way that the discovery of the pearl is at once the focal point of the story told in *Hymn of the Pearl* and strangely unimportant to it (it is not mentioned again after the prince succeeds in acquiring it; its acquisition is important because it merges with the garment), so the green girdle is important only at the moment of its acquisition, for the gnosis it entails frees Gawain from the material world and renders him indestructible. It would be superfluous and, in a sense, impossible for the Green Knight to demand the return of the girdle. It represents a path that can be trod in only one direction. Its acquisition by Gawain is the poet's metaphor for his acquisition of sensitivity toward his own being, his own self. It saves him from death in two ways. On the prosaic level it saves him from the axe of the Green Knight, and on the more profound, metaphysical level, it saves him from death by enlightening him regarding the immortality of the soul and the irrelevance of the death of the flesh. The tale is one of revelation and enlightenment rather than salvation or instant redemption. The story is not about grace so much as about gnosis, intuitive knowledge in matters of the spirit.

In a sense, then, Gawain's story is a gnostic tale no less than the story of the prince and the pearl. We can return now to the latter story to see how it ends. When we left it, the garment was about to speak. This is what it has to say:

> *I am the Active of Deeds,*
> *Who they reared for him in my father's presence*
> *And I also perceived in myself*
> *That my stature was growing in accord with his labors.*[29]

This is the Iranian concept of the heavenly soul (celestial *daena*), which reunites with the earthly soul a few days after death. The daena is made beautiful or ugly by the deeds performed by the bearer of the soul during his or her sojourn on earth. In an old Avestan text, the daena explains how the system works:

> *I was lovely and you made me more lovely*
> *I was beautiful and you made me more beautiful.*
> *I was desirable and you made me more desirable....*
> *Through this good thought, through this good work,*
> *through this good deed.*[30]

The symbolism might be a bit obscure, but the basic principle is clear enough: by donning his cloak, the prince paves the path for his personal redemption.[31]

Finally, the prince does unite with his daena:

> *And in its kingly motions*
> *It was spreading itself out towards me,*
> *And in the hands of its givers*
> *It hastened that I might take it.*

And me too my love urged on
That I should run to meet it and receive it
And I stretched forth and received it
With the beauty of its colors I adorned myself....[32]

So the prince does find redemption, just as the Jew does when he wraps himself up in the tallit first thing each morning and declares, with hopefulness: "In Your light, we shall see light."[33]

The Jew at morning prayer dons the tallit as an essentially redemptive act grounded in metaphor and seasoned with a bit of magic. The tallit symbolizes, first, the soul, for the daily return of which one is bidden liturgically to offer thanks to God, the Source of all life. This is the simplest level of interpretive thought, reflected in the fact that *modeh ani* traditionally is considered to be a child's prayer. There is, however, another level hovering just above the metaphoric ~ the plane of sympathetic magic. God has a cloak as well, one woven with the soul of the Jewish people, one that functions as the very soul of God.[34] The Jew at worship dons the tallit in an act of pre-emptive *imitatio Dei*. The donning of the soul-cloak by God is considered symbolic of the coming redemption and must be triggered from below by a nation enwrapped in its own salvific garment.

Metaphor is the realm of reality in which all existents may identify and trade places with their equivalents. It is well within the metaphoric universe that Judaism functions ritually best. On the most basic level of symbol and myth, the Jew who wraps himself in his tallit is acting in direct imitation of God, thereby fulfilling the most primary longing of religious man: to be holy and to be like God. By so doing, he demonstrates his faith in the doctrine of God the Creator, and willingness and intent to create a private universe of symbol, metaphor, and myth, with and in which to serve the divine paradigm. On a slightly higher level, the idea is even more potent: to do not only as God does but as one wishes God to do. To worship the Redeemer of Israel, Israel can do no less than bring about its own redemption.

---

[1] The requirement to wear fringes on garments is stated in the Torah in Numbers (15:38-39), where the Hebrew term is *tzitzit*, and in Deuteronomy (22:12), where the term is *gedilim*. Whatever the original distinction, Rabbinic sources took for granted that both terms refer to the same type of ritual fringe. Both terms have other meanings as well. *Gedilim* in I Kings 7:17 refers to the decoration at the capital of a column. *Tzitzit* in Ezekiel 8:3 appears to refer to a lock of hair. The earliest compendium of laws relating to the tallit is *Massekhet Tzitzit*, published with translation into English by Michael Higger in his *Seven Minor Tractates* (New York, 1930, reprinted in Jerusalem in 1971), pp. 50-52 (Hebrew) and pp. 31-33 (English). These laws are supplemented by Maimonides in his *Mishneh Torah, Sefer Ahavah*, where he addresses the question of the artificial way in which the commandment generally is performed. Cf. the remarks of *Hagahot Maimuniot, ad locum*.

[2] Theodor Reik, *Pagan Rites in Judaism* (New York, 1944), pp. 103-152, especially 141-146. The animal is presumably a bull or a

calf, in accordance with the narrative of the golden calf in Exodus and the description of the sanctuary at Beth El in the days of Jeroboam. Both Aaron and Jeroboam are quoted by Scripture as declaring, "This is your God, O Israel, who took you out of the land of Egypt," as they contemplated the bovine statues they themselves had erected. Cf. Exodus 32:4 and I Kings 12:28.

[3] Psalms 36:10.

[4] Psalms 104:2.

[5] Cf. V. Aptowitzer, *Zur Kosmologie der Aggadah: Licht als Urstoff,* *MGW7,* N.S. 36 (1928), pp. 363-390; Altmann, "Gnostic Themes in Rabbinic Cosmology," in *Essays in Honour of the Very Rev. Dr. J. H. Hertz,* ed. Epstein, Levine, and Roth (London, 1943), pp. 28-32; and Altmann, "A Note on the Rabbinic Doctrine of Creation," JJS 7 (1956), pp. 195-206. Cf. also R. Lowe, "The Divine Garment and the Shi'ur Qomah," *Harvard Theological Review* 58 (1965), pp. 153-166.

[6] According to this line of thinking, the garment, a special article of clothing that suggests the wearer's position in society, becomes a type of outer shell of the person involved, and thus at the same time becomes a handy parallel to the image of the soul or the self, of which the flesh itself is an outer layer or shell. This is the province of metaphor, a process of thought and expression, rooted in the idea of creative misanalysis, whereby things merely juxtaposed in some way with each other are seen as integrally connected.

[7] Genesis 39:12-19.

[8] *Bereishit Rabbah* 87:7, ed. Theodor-Albeck, p. 1073. Some manuscripts refer specifically to the garment that Joseph left behind.

⁹ The decisive element here is magic. Once magic is involved, especially sympathetic magic, there can be no use of simile, because the whole notion of sympathetic magic presumes in the first place that we are able to transcend mere comparison and to discover and assert the kind of new inner relationships and connections that themselves transcend the physical universe and its regular laws. Magic takes the same role in the physical world that metaphor takes in the world of literary expression. Magic presumes metaphor, just as metaphor, to the extent it is taken seriously, suggests magic. In this particular case, metaphor is the key to the essential unity of the sea, the bones, and the garment. As the metaphors that sustain these truths fall away, and the three become more overtly and obviously one, the reader is introduced to a secret and becomes privy to an esoteric aspect of the nature of things. The fates of the three elements intertwine in the perception of the listener, who soon becomes aware of the fact that affecting one may effect change in another. This is the basic definition of magic. Sympathetic magic is the science of applying metaphor to physical reality.

¹⁰ This is the translation of Hans Jonas as published in his *The Gnostic Religion* (Boston, 1963), p. 114. I have changed a word or two based upon my own understanding of the Syriac.

¹¹ A. A. Bevan, *The Hymn of the Soul* (Cambridge, 1897), pp. 24f.

¹² Jonas, p. 125.

¹³ Mark 15:24 and parallels.

¹⁴ Luke 23:11, Matthew 27:28, 31. Cf. Mark 15:17-20.
¹⁵ Luke 23:24, Matthew 27:35-36, Mark 15:24. Cf. John 19:23-24, where it is specifically stated that lots were drawn so that the undergarment, which had no seams, would not be ripped to pieces. The outer cloak was divided into four parts so that one part could be given to each of the four soldiers. This elaboration

of the basic myth seems to have been prompted by midrashic considerations rooted in the early Christian exegesis of Psalms 22:18.

[16] For example, the prayer *modeh ani*: I am grateful to You, living, enduring King, for restoring my soul to me in compassion. You are faithful beyond measure. (*Siddur Sim Shalom*, ed. Harlow, p. 3.)

[17] II Moses 118-120, ed. Loeb Classical Library (Cambridge, Massachusetts and London, 1966), pp. 504-507.

[18] Koran 74:1, trans. Arberry (London and New York, 1955), volume two, p. 310.

[19] Koran 73: 1, trans. op. cit., p. 308.

[20] Jeremiah 13:1-3.

[21] Jeremiah 13:3-9.

[22] Jeremiah 13:11.

[23] Psalms 104:2.

[24] Mishnah *Hagigah* 2:2.

[25] *Bereishit Rabbah* 3:4, ed. Theodor-Albeck, pp. 19f.

[26] *Hekhalot Rabbati* 3:4, trans. Gershom Scholem, in *Jewish Gnosticism, Merkabah Mysticism and Talmudic Tradition*, second ed. (New York, 1965), pp. 59-60.

[27] One of the most famous hymns to emanate from the circle of those ancient mystics is the one which is to be sung once a year, on the morning of the Day of Atonement, *Ha'aderet Veha'emunah*,

the beginning of which declares: "The cloak and the faith, these are for Him who is everlasting." Anyone who has read Agnon's story *Tallit Aheret* ("Another Tallit") will not be unacquainted with the dire consequences that even slighting the hymn (let alone the Deity who wears the cloak it describes) can carry for one who arrives too late in the synagogue service to hear it sung.

[28] *Sir Gawain and the Green Knight*, ed. Stone (Middlesex and Baltimore, 1959), Chapter 63, p. 97.

[29] *Hymn of the Soul (=Hymn of the Pearl)*, ed. cit., p. 29.

[30] Yasht 22:14.

[31] The Jews of Babylonia knew of the daena and used that notion to explain the phenomenon of existential, unexplained terror, panic or anxiety. No individual could see and thus no individual could recognize the source of his or her fears, but the individual's daena could. The twist here, in the Babylonian Jewish context, is that the daena is identified with the stars and is called *mazal* (literally "constellation"), a word that later came to mean "luck" or "fortune" in a progression of meaning that is both obvious and rather optimistic.

[32] *Hymn of the Soul*, ed. cit., p. 29.

[33] Psalms 36:10. Cf. Job 24:13-16, where God Himself is called light.

[34] Can one translate the opening lines of the *Nishmat* prayer to yield the idea that the soul of the ever living God (i.e., Israel) shall (now) praise the name of God?

Tekhelet ~ A Royal Reminder
Mordecai M. Kaplan

A significant keynote of the Torah is found in
מִצְוַת צִיצִת (*mitzvat tzitzit*):

> "When you look upon these fringes, you will be
> reminded of all the commandments of Adonai
> and fulfill them."

וְנָתְנוּ עַל־צִיצִת הַכָּנָף פְּתִיל תְּכֵלֶת

(*V'natnu al tzitzit hakanaf petil tekhelet.*)

Where is the תְּכֵלֶת (*tekhelet*)? Why don't we have it?
Did you ever ask yourself this question? And how
many congregations have this pointed out to them?

Of course, all of us are taught that the reason we have
no תְּכֵלֶת (*tekhelet*) today is that there is no longer
hilazon for the dye. But that is a very fishy reason. I
think that Jews have been ashamed to give the real

reason for no longer having תְּכֵלֶת (*tekhelet*), and that is why this fishy reason was advanced.

The real reason (and here I would indulge in the kind interpretation that we had the privilege of hearing from Professor Finkelstein this morning) is that the Roman government issued a prohibition against using תְּכֵלֶת (*tekhelet*). Under Roman law, anyone other than royalty who wore תְּכֵלֶת (*tekhelet*), the sign of royalty, was executed. One dared not wear anything that implied he did not recognize the supreme sovereignty of the Roman emperor.

"When you look upon these fringes you will be reminded of all the commandments of Adonai and fulfill them. You will not be led astray by the inclinations of your heart or the allurements of your eyes. Then you will remember and fulfill all My commandments and be holy before Your God." We have here the motivation for controlling that which leads to lawlessness ~ passions and desires, which we must learn to control. How? Through דֶּרֶךְ הַשֵּׁם (*derekh Hashem*), through the laws. And how do you remind yourself? Look not at the צִיצת (*tzitzit*) but at the tekhelet, at the blue, at the purple, and in doing so you will recall that you have a מֶלֶךְ (*melekh* - king). Having a מֶלֶךְ (*melekh*), and knowing it, you no longer give in to your passions, for you follow laws.

To Wear Tzitzit
Nina Beth Cardin

Speak to the Israelite people and instruct them to make for themselves fringes on the corners of their garments throughout the ages; let them attach a cord of blue to the fringe at each corner. (Numbers 15:40)

The *mitzvah of tzitzit* (the ritual fringes attached to the four corners of the tallit) offers us one of the richest metaphors for Torah, God and the Jewish people.

The צִיצִת (*tzitzit*) themselves represent the Jewish people. Though we are strengthened in our being woven together, each of us alone is a fragile thread. We are threatened with being blown away by the whim of wind and time. Yet through the knots and bindings of the *mitzvah of tzitzit,* through our social, emotional, spiritual and historical ties with those around us, we are joined to the sturdier presence of others. What was insubstantial now becomes substantial. What was a wisp now becomes a defining edge of something greater.

That something greater is Torah, the cloth that binds all Jews. The complex juncture of צִיצָת (*tzitzit*) to the cloth reveals the complex juncture of Jews to Torah, and to other Jews. Just as the cloth is incomplete without the צִיצָת (*tzitzit*) to frame and hallow it, so the Torah is incomplete without the Jews to define it and, yes, hallow it.

And just as the fringes sometimes seem disparate one from the other, one grouping on this end and another grouping on that end, so too do the Jews sometimes seem hopelessly disparate and apart. Yet, like the צִיצָת (*tzitzit*), no matter how far apart we seem, we are all bound to each other by the same cloth of Torah.

And where in all this is God? God is, as it were, like the תְּכֵלֶת (*tekhelet*), the blue thread whose dye we no longer have. The significance of the צִיצָת (*tzitzit*) resides not in themselves, but in their proximity to and context for the blue thread. So, too, the significance of the Jews in their relationship to God. Just as the blue thread was once evident to the Jews, God's presence was once more evident. And just as the blue thread is now hidden to us, so is God hidden.

But we remain the bearers of the stories of God; we remain the reminder of the presence of God, even as the צִיצָת (*tzitzit*) are the bearers of the story of the blue thread, and an enduring reminder of its presence.

We begin the שְׁמַע (*Sh'ma*) ~ the daily liturgy in which we recite the laws of צִיצָת (*tzitzit*) ~ with a reminder of and a call for God's unity in the presence of Israel. We end with a call for and a reminder of Israel's unity in the presence of God.

A Union of Weavers
Nina Beth Cardin

We Jews are a union of weavers. Interlacing our traditions and languages, our rituals and laws, with fibers gathered from cultures around us, we each weave a personal shawl of Judaism. Some shawls are open and loose, allowing the currents of other cultures to flow in and out easily. Others are fine and tight, holding much of Jewish culture in and foreign cultures out.

The world of Judaism is filled with shawls of different weaves, from loose to fine, filtering the larger world in or out to a greater or lesser degree. Each adds its flair, its strength, and its warmth to the sacred garment of the Jewish people. Our choice of weave determines where we worship, what we eat, where we live, how we pray, whom we marry, what we do in our spare time, and how we educate our children. And every now and then we add a thread or two of a new hue and a new texture that serves to enrich and extend our wardrobe.

Sadly, sometimes we derogate one another's craftsmanship. It is true that with too loose a weave the cloth loses its integrity and ceases to be. And it is also true that with too tight a weave the body underneath smothers and dies. But most of our shawls fall somewhere in between. They complement one another, reflect in their similarity of form one another's authenticity, preserve the secrets of the different weaves for one another and for future generations, which is very good, for no one shawl can suit every Jew. And yet while we weavers differ, we should acknowledge that we all work on the same loom, with the same warp holding tight our differing patterns of weft. And that, if nothing else, should unite us.

Judaism offers three interwoven strategies to help us remain conscious of the artistry of everyday living, three ways for us to open ourselves to the holiness of the everyday: prayers, blessings, and sacred deeds. Prayers and blessings are the verbal pauses we insert in the course of our everyday; words that focus our awareness and our appreciation, words we say before *or* after an act or a moment of discovery. Sacred deeds are moral, ritual or social acts that anchor and secure our masterpiece.

Formal Prayers ~

To immerse ourselves in the prayers of the everyday is to shed the perspective of self that might restrict us and enslave us. We are invited to don the cloak of community that enlarges us and encompasses us. As sociologists and psychologists tell us, the surest and most satisfying way to self is through the corridors of community. "It is within society, and as a result of social processes," Peter Berger writes in The *Sacred Canopy,* "that the individual becomes a person, that he attains and holds onto an identity; and that he carries out the various projects that constitute his life." Liturgical prayer, especially conducted within the context of community, is one place where self becomes.

Perhaps that is part of my romance with the tallit, the prayer shawl that adult Jews drape around themselves during morning prayers. When I put on a tallit, even when I am alone, I place myself in the folds of my people. Donning the tallit is a daily, visual symbol of my identity; reminding me to whom I belong as I begin my day's journey. It protects me, shields me and defines me. Falling around my shoulders and arms, the tallit provides me with a secure awareness of my body and its boundaries. I am not lost there, but found. Others are outside, I am inside, but we are one. I fill up my tallit. No matter my size, I always will. And it is in that fullness that I am counted as a member of the congregation.

These two domains ~ the personal and the communal ~ are not distinct; rather, they meld into each other. I cannot be who I am without my community nor can my community be what it is without me. Rabbi Arthur Waskow tells how the tallit is a symbol of this melding: The corners of the tallit are not sharp and precise but *edged* with צִיצָת (*tzitzit*), the fringe mandated by the text of the Torah. The fringe, the woolen threads, represent how the boundaries of the community and those of the individual open themselves to one another every day.

Some of our prayers are formal, with words set by the hand of tradition. You can find them in daily and holiday prayer books. We say those prayers at designated times, either alone or with a minyan (a group of at least ten adult Jews). Those formal prayers weave together the needs and the dreams of the Jewish community with those of its individual members. Whatever our personal needs, we are always also members of the Jewish people, sharing in our people's joy and pain. So three times a day every day of the year it is the tradition of some Jews to say those prayers on behalf of ourselves and our community, the people Israel.

The Tallit in Stories

Another Tallit
S. Y. Agnon
Translated by Jules Harlow

About my other prayer shawls I have already told. So now I merely add what happened on Yom Kippur with the tallit which I had left in the synagogue of my grandfather, may he rest in peace.

That Yom Kippur, I had the notion to pray with my grandfather. Because I lived far from the synagogue and because I had stayed in bed too long that morning, I arrived after the chanting of Pesukei Dezimra. This is truly regrettable, for on Yom Kippur, at my grandfather's synagogue, they recite this part of the service verse by verse, in a special chant. Already in my childhood, before I knew the meaning of the words, whenever the cantor wrapped his tallit around his face and chanted Chei Haolamim, I would be perplexed, for the cantor called to Him in a loud voice even though He was right there! Why did he cover his face? If he uncovered his face, the whole world would be filled with a great joy such as I felt when I played hide-and-seek with my father. We used to look for each other until, finally, I would uncover my face, and then we found each other.

When I entered the synagogue, my grandfather brought his face out of the folds of his tallit, and turned here and there, searching out a seat for me in the synagogue which was already filled with worshippers. By the east wall, to the right of my grandfather, sat a group of old men, each looking different from all the others and, it goes without saying, from other men in general. Their faces were wrinkled like raisins, their beards looked like cinnamon sticks. Their eyes which had no lashes were bloodshot, yet from their eyes there streamed a joy so substantial you could feel it with your hands. How did they all come to be in one place, in my grandfather's synagogue, and why were their features so different? One of them, who understood what my grandfather wanted of him, answered in Aramaic: "The law for Yom Kippur is not like that of Passover which states that all who want can sit and eat." To paraphrase his statement in terms of the matter at hand, we might say, "Today I am not obliged to be pushed around to furnish a seat for one who has none."

I was disturbed that my grandfather should be troubled on my account and I said to him, "Please, do not bother about me. I shall find a place for myself." I was just talking. This was his synagogue and he could find no place for me. How could I find a seat by myself? However, my grandfather was troubled not only because there was no place for me, but because I had come so late. I deliberated: perhaps I should tell him that I prayed the morning service at the synagogue in my neighborhood. But it is not nice for one to make his grandfather a cause for telling lies. Because of the crowding and the heat and the candles and the great number of worshippers, the roof of my mouth was dry. Leibel, the Zaddik's grandson, came over to me. "Come with me," he said. I didn't know why he asked me to go with him, but I was drawn to him, so I went.

When he had brought me to his house, he left me in the hall, and came back with a pitcher which he offered me to sniff at, so that my burning thirst should be eased.

I took the pitcher in both my hands and brought it up to my nose, all the while amazed: why did he fill the pitcher with fruit juice? Couldn't he find a little water? Leibel's blank face showed no desire to answer my questions. Meanwhile, the juice in the pitcher actually began to froth up toward my teeth. I sucked in my lips to shield my teeth from the fruit juice. But it continued bubbling up from the lip of the pitcher to my lips, frothing around my nose, gushing up to bring its taste to my mouth. I was filled with anger at Leibel. I seized him and dragged him after me, and it

looked as though we were walking together. When
we reached the synagogue, my grandfather again
gave me a troubled glance. Could he have sensed
what had happened? I acted as if there were some
other explanation.

"You are upset because I stand here without a tallit
on. I'll get my tallit, the one that's here in your
synagogue, and wrap myself in it right away."

I looked up to see if he was satisfied, and I saw that
they had brought benches into the synagogue and
placed them to the left of the Holy Ark, one on top of
the other, like the steps of a bathhouse. A man whose
name I do not wish to mention was standing on the
top step, wearing some type of baker's hat, and
chanting hymns which were not from the Yom
Kippur service. A small boy ~ his son or grandson ~
stood at his side, accompanying the hymns with
foolish gesticulations. Half the congregation was
smiling at them. How did they get here? And when
did they get here? Meanwhile, they stepped down
and went away. "What is this?" I asked myself.
"When my grandfather was looking for a place for
me, why didn't he look to the left of the Ark? There
were many benches and many empty places there.
And then again, how could that man leave in the
middle of services, and where did he go?"

My grandfather looked at me. Suddenly I reached
into a hole in a table and brought out my tallit. I had

often looked for my tallit there without finding it, but now I found it. Unless you say that someone else had taken it and then returned it, it is an amazing thing indeed.

As I prepared to wrap myself in my tallit, I saw that one of the fringes was missing. A certain fellow whom we usually ignore though he never ignores us whispered to me: "Your tallit has only three fringes." I began deliberating: what is he telling me? Don't I know that a tallit with only three fringes cannot be used? Or did he want to remind me of a forgotten tradition: while a man is alive, even though he may be holding a tallit of three fringes in his hand, he is not allowed to wear it. But when he is dead, they pursue him with a proper tallit of four fringes, pluck out one fringe, and force him to wear it.

Depression overcame me. Not because of what had been whispered to me, but because of this holy day of Yom Kippur which had passed by without a prayer, without anything.

A Stranger's Tallit
Allan Rabinowitz

On Simhat Torah, at the small egalitarian synagogue I attend in Jerusalem, I sat near the table on which the Torah lay open. As is our tradition, the children were called forward for a collective blessing, beneath a tallit spread over them as a canopy. I removed mine, which is huge. As we held it above those children I turned to my wife and saw that she had tears in her eyes, as I suddenly did.

For an old woman named Chava gave me that tallit more than twenty years earlier when, as a yeshiva student in Jerusalem, I lived in a block-like stucco apartment complex. My kitchen window looked across the rubble-filled central courtyard into hers. Often I saw her enter her kitchen and take her bright flowered apron off its hook. With round cheeks, wire glasses and a bun of silver hair, she looked like a picture on a cookie package. My roommate Glenn and I nicknamed her Mrs. Fields.

In my first exchange with her, on the stairs, she said that, "when you hang your laundry out it drips on the laundry of the woman below. Check first before you hang it." We were just one more set of students who wandered through this apartment.

Colorful prints hung on her kitchen's eggshell-colored wall. Every Friday evening, on a little cabinet against the wall, she lit Shabbat candles. Occasionally, as Chava glided through the creamy kitchen light, I envied that bubble of comfort and order, which sharply contrasted with our eternally dish-filled sink. Among the courtyard debris beneath Chava's window, cats gathered everyday at dusk, and jockeyed for position with yowling, hissing, and claw strikes. They tautened when she slid her kitchen window open, and sprang forward and up when she tossed out a daily ration of food scraps.

Glenn and I studied at the yeshiva all day. Glenn diligently awoke early every morning for *shacharit* prayers at school before classes began. But I resisted prayer, and wrote in the early hours. One cold, dark winter morning, just after Glenn left, there was a hard pounding on my door. As I opened it, Chava frantically beckoned me to follow her.

When we entered her neat apartment she tugged me by my sleeve to the bathroom and gestured for me to open the door. But something blocked it. Wiggling it back and forth, I was able at last to thrust my head past the doorjamb. To my surprise, an old, heavy man with bulging eyes, clutching his heart and gasping, slumped against the door in pajamas. He must have been confined to bed all this time. I told Chava to call for an ambulance, and futilely practiced the little CPR technique I remembered from a first-aid course. In the living room, a neighbor named Rachel comforted Chava as she wept.

The ambulance driver asked me to help carry the man down the stairs in a wheelchair. I grabbed its front end. The sick man wore an oxygen mask. As I backed gingerly down the stairs, he labored for breath. His belly bulged out of a partially unbuttoned pajama shirt. His hair was wispy and gray, highlighting jagged black eyebrows. Above the mask, large blue eyes fixed upon my eyes. Those eyes closed before we reached the ambulance.

Later that day, Rachel knocked on my door and told me that the man never re-opened his eyes, and died on the way to the hospital. From the front seat, Chava had heard the paramedic's efforts to revive him. I, a stranger, was the last person this man saw.

The many neighbors who made *shiva* calls to Chava were mostly old and hunched. When I visited in the evening, there was hardly space to sit. The room was stuffy and warm, despite the harsh winds outside. One wall was lined with shelves filled with volumes of the Talmud, the Torah with commentaries, and additional religious texts. A breakfront on another wall was filled with painted plates, cups, and delicate porcelain animals.

Chava sat on a cushion on the floor. She looked at me and nodded, then leaned over and whispered something to a young man who sat beside her. He looked to be a few years older than me, with wild dark curls that obscured his small kippah. He wore brown slippers, and his plaid shirt had been ripped near the collar.

He rose and approached me. "I'm Avi, the son," he said in English with a gurgling Israeli accent. I offered condolences, in Hebrew. He nodded. "Where you from in the States?" he asked, again in English.

"New Jersey."

"Really? I'm in New York."

"How long are you there for?"

He shrugged. "I'm just there. I'm a painter." From his back pocket he pulled a business card, with his name and studio address written in blue brush-stroked letters. "When you come back, come visit my studio. I have some shows coming up."

"Thanks. I'm not sure when I'll be back."

"Neither am I." A heavyset woman cut between us and engulfed him in her arms as she sniffled out her sorrow.

Someone asked me to come to an early minyan the next morning for shacharit prayers, and before thinking I said I would. When I showed up the next morning, Chava, in slippers and a ripped housedress, was sitting on her cushion sipping tea.

Men wrapped tefillin on their arms, each man draped in a tallit. Avi stood there wearing neither, only a kippah, like me. Thus far, I did not wear tefillin, and did not own a tallit. If Avi had not been there, I would have felt like an imposter. Even so, I expected to be accosted or scolded.

Chava brought over a tallit, in a beautiful blue velvet bag, and I used that. I was surprised that she brought it to me, rather than to her son. After the prayers, a man quietly offered me his tefillin. I accepted, let him wrap them on my arm, said the blessings, then removed them.

I showed up every morning for prayers. Chava handed me the tallit, and the same man offered his tefillin after he finished praying. They felt unwieldy on me, yet in the tallit I felt embraced in a membrane that enhanced the power of the words.

Avi left immediately after the seven-day shiva period.
I again saw Chava puttering around her kitchen. One
morning she again knocked on my door. "I have
something for you," she said. "Please come." In her
apartment, again neatly arranged, we sat at a small
nicked table in the kitchen. She offered me tea, and
served it with cookies. Then she excused herself, left
the room, and returned a moment later carrying a
white plastic bag.

"Moshe was a real Torah scholar," she said as she sat
again. "He would study fourteen, fifteen hours a day.
Students took turns studying with him. Like dancing
partners." I felt awkward as she rambled. "Sometimes
I put a cup of tea by him and he never noticed until I
said, 'Moshele, your tea's getting cold.' Then he
would look up, with his eyes so wide like they just
wanted to drink in every word in the book, and cock
his head. Like a puppy." I pictured those blue eyes
facing me, drinking in only fear.

"In the Thirties, students gathered around him in
basements, secretly; Stalin already hunted religious
Jews. Finally he and our first son ~ Ya'acov ~ landed
in work camps in Siberia. I didn't even know Moshe
was still alive until 1949. I was walking along Jaffa
Road, and a man before me was walking so slowly,
with a book open before him. Then he cocked his
head, and I cried out, 'Dear God, it's Moshe.' He
turned, and we both screamed there on the sidewalk.
That's when I learned that Ya'acov had died in a labor

camp, and I cried over him as if I had never thought that before."

That was an amazing story, I mumbled, and beautiful. "Not so beautiful, believe me," she said. "I hated this place. Some of Moshe's old students wanted to bring him to New York to teach. But he said he was staying here, no matter what. 'No matter what?' I asked him. 'So that another son should die? It's better if he dies in uniform?'" She smiled. "My son's in New York now. He's a painter."

"Yes, he told me."

"He wants me to go there," she said.

"And are you going?"

She shrugged and put down her tea. "Oh, Moshe was so hurt that Avi dropped kashrut and Shabbat, after what he'd gone through just to be here. He kept reminding him of how Ya'acov always studied. I said to Moshe, 'You think we can influence these young ones? Forget it, that's the way things are.'"

She reached into the white plastic bag and pulled out the embroidered blue velvet bag containing the tallit I had been praying in all week. "I thought I'd give this to Avi. But he'd probably use it to clean his brushes. You're the only one beside my husband who's ever worn it."

In shock, I took and stroked the bag, barely able to thank her. Enveloped in this broad tallit, which belonged to a man I never knew, yet whose eyes I saw staring into death, I had prayed to open to God. And now it was pressed upon me.

Before the next Shabbat, I bought flowers for Chava. She protested, then profusely thanked me. Later I saw the flowers, from across the courtyard, standing in a vase on her kitchen counter, opposite my window. It struck me as a strange place to display flowers.

I still had Avi's business card. I wrote to him that I had his father's tallit; it was his for the asking. "Thanks, I'll keep that in mind," he answered. "If you visit New Jersey, come see my studio." He never did request the tallit, and I never saw his studio.

I saw Chava passing on the stairs, puttering in her kitchen, feeding the cats. When I offered to pick up odd items for her at the nearby grocery, or to move heavy objects in her apartment, she refused my offer with thanks and smiles. And she never invited me again for tea, during all those following months that I plunged into Jewish sources and learned to pray.

Sometimes, wrapped in my tallit, I imagined him rocking in it saying the same prayers, his blue eyes bright and fervent. This tallit spread over my bride and me as a *huppah*, and surrounded my son after his *brit milah*.

He was among the gaggle of kids who approached the Torah under it. Next Simhat Torah, I will make certain that I again sit in the front.

My Father's Tallit and the Sefer Torah
Ruthy Bodner

Recently, my husband and I had the privilege of our son becoming a bar mitzvah. To celebrate with friends and relatives and to put more מִצְוָה (*mitzvah*) in his bar mitzvah, we dedicated a Sefer Torah to our shul in memory of my father and my husband's grandfather and of course in honor of our son's bar mitzvah.

While planning this event, and detailing the Torah's every move, I was informed that a חֻפָּה (*huppah*) and four poles would be held over the people taking turns holding the Torah as they walked from our house to the shul. The Torah would be treated as a bridegroom, escorted under the חֻפָּה (*huppah*). The other Torahs would be taken out of the Aron Kodesh to greet the new Torah to their home, the shul and their Ark, the Torah's resting place. Music and dancing would take place, and the festivities evolve into a very moving ceremony.

It got me thinking. My father passed away six years before, and since we were honoring his memory, wouldn't it be nice to use his tallit as the חֻפָּה (*huppah*) for the Torah? My husband called my mother and she too was excited and moved. However, after six years, she had just recently moved into an apartment and had finally parted with some of my father's things ~ and the tallit was one of them! After so many years, she had decided to donate the tallit to her shul.

She immediately called her shul and asked them if they still had her husband's tallit. They did, and that day she was able to pick it up and bring it back to her home for safekeeping. When she arrived in my home in Teaneck, NJ it was evident that it was my father's tallit. It was old and yellow, not new and white.

My son posed for pictures wearing the tallit and holding the Torah. It was so moving to watch the חֻפָּה (*huppah*) go up and wait for its bridegroom, our Torah.

Nothing prepared me for the spiritual fulfillment of finishing the letters of a Torah in our home and escorting it out into the street, watching it pass from one good friend and relative to another as they walked under my father's tallit. I was in a fragile emotional state, teetering on tears yet accepting people's good cheer and wishes of Mazel Tov ~ Mazel Tov, not just on my son's impending Bar Mitzvah, but also for finishing a Torah, mitzvah number 613. I caught a few friends' teary eyes as they watched the procession, and it made me feel so good and special, partaking in such a fundamentally Jewish act. My father's tallit serving as the canopy escorting this Torah made it all the more meaningful and powerful to our family. We really felt his presence. The Torah was for him, and he was bringing it home.

The Babies' Aliyah in Jerusalem
Judith Weisberg

In Orthodox synagogues on Simhat Torah it is customary for all the men and boys to ascend the bimah to make a blessing over the last Chapter of the Torah. In my shul in Jerusalem, immediately after the last four-year-old has finished stammering the unfamiliar words, his father's tallit (prayer shawl) hanging from his tiny shoulders, the fathers rush to pick up their babies and toddlers, who are too young for this ritual, and disappear with them under a roof of six or seven prayer shawls held together. This is called the "babies' aliyah," or the "pacifier get-together," a joint blessing for the very young.

We mothers are glued to the mehitzah (partition) separating us from the men, not wanting to miss the scene.

As a blond pony-tailed youngster held in his father's arms peeks out from underneath the stark contrasting black and white of the tallit, Jewish past, present, and future flow together in the emotions of most onlookers. The children are so very young and vulnerable, and Jewish history, while beautiful, is so brutal.

The mind's eye recollects other husbands, fathers, brothers wrapped in these very same prayer shawls while being buried alive, shot, tortured, and massacred so long ago by the Romans and so recently by the Nazis. These tallitot both covered and betrayed Jewish loyalists pursued by Torquemada and Stalin, Titus and the Hellenists.

No other garment in history is more characteristic, symbolic, and bloodstained than these pieces of white wool striped with black.

A Jew wrapped in his tallit is no longer simply Mitch Riedman, the baker, or Alan Gold, the stockbroker. From the front, his face is almost hidden, and from the rear he appears nearly identical to his "colleagues"; without any other distracting colors, he has become a member of a timeless army, whether he feels like a soldier or not.

In the women's balcony, the mothers shiver. They try to detect their own sons, but they also watch the sum of all those innocent feet and curls, the sticky little hands holding bags with pretzels and chewing gum, the round-eyed faces brown with chocolate, like the shirts that started out white this morning.

"I have given before you life and death," I hear our mother quote the Torah. She is praying fiercely: "We want life, God. I know we have pledged our children to you. When you asked at Mount Sinai how we would guarantee our loyalty to the Torah, the only assurance you would accept was our babies. We have lost so many of them," she cries now. "We have lost so many of these precious ones." This Israeli mother is the daughter of a Holocaust survivor. She has also witnessed the bombing of a Jerusalem bus. She presses a tissue against her face, while clutching a little girl with her other arm. "Please, God, help us to remain loyal, and let us celebrate their birthdays, and let all of us dance at their weddings."

Zayde's Tallit
Karen Misler

I don't have very many memories of my grandfather, Jacob Siegel, as he died when I was three years old. When Barry and I got engaged and began to plan our wedding, I became aware that my older brother Michael had my zayde's tallit. I thought that using it as my huppah would be a wonderful way to bring in a connection to generations that had gone before us, so I asked to borrow it.

Several years later, as I approached my 40th birthday, I was looking for a meaningful way to mark this milestone. My father had died a few years before, and I knew that one of his regrets was that he never had a formal bar mitzvah. As I had spent my childhood attending an Orthodox synagogue, I had never had a bat mitzvah either. So I decided to celebrate my special birthday with an adult bat mitzvah that I dedicated to my father's memory. To make it that much more special, I once again borrowed my zayde's tallit to wear for the occasion.

I do not normally wear a tallit during services, but I felt truly cloaked in tradition as I stood on the bimah and recited the maftir aliyah and the haftorah. In my speech, I noted that I might be one of the few women in history who had used the same tallit as both a huppah and for her bat mitzvah ~ and in that order!

A few years later, as our son Jeremy's bar mitzvah approached, I knew that I wanted to include the same tallit once more. Yet, on a family trip to Israel a few years before, Jeremy had picked out his own tallit. We agreed that he would wear my zayde's tallit during his leyning. Because Jeremy is named for his great-grandfather, we all felt that seeing him wrapped in that tallit would add a special element of continuity to an already very special occasion. As Jeremy stood proudly on the bimah that day, I could almost feel my zayde looking down from heaven and smiling his approval and his joy.

After Jeremy's Bar Mitzvah, my brother told me that he thought the tallit belonged in my care, and so it waits in my house for the next important family occasion. Perhaps we will have the pleasure of seeing it used for Jeremy's own wedding.

Tallit: Wings of Shekhinah
Susan Mitrani Knapp

A few years ago, I decided to daven outside one beautiful crisp fall morning. It was probably during Sukkot, since I like to pray in the sukkah. I remember putting on my tallit and stretching my arms out from my body, horizontally, like wings. It seemed as if my arms with the tallit over them were like כַּנְפֵי שְׁכִינָה (kanfei Shekhinah) ~ the wings of the שְׁכִינָה (Shekhinah), and they were there to protect me.

Then, I *thought* about the wings. Recently, I *used* them to fly ~ spiritually.

In 5765, I took a position as student rabbi and led my first High Holy Day services. I worked hard to prepare myself spiritually during the month of Elul, and felt ready to serve the congregation as their spiritual leader. When I was on the בִּימָה (bima) I was fully present to God's presence. I felt that I was following the flow of God's intention. I realized that I was not under the wings of the שְׁכִינָה (*Shekhinah*) for protection, but that I was using them to fly in a spiritual sense.

The tallit enabled me to use these wings much as a bird uses its wings. Birds don't think too much about the air current, but use their instincts and intuition to fly at the current that is just right to get them where they need to go. That's what I was doing. In a spiritual sense, I was holding my arms out to catch the divine flow of energy, and these "wings" helped me soar close to God.

After the service, a woman approached me. She told me that she has been engaged for a number of years, but her Jewish fiancé had not been supportive of her commitment to Judaism. She said that something shifted for him during this service, and that he came away with a real understanding of what the tradition meant to her.

I told her this was the work of God. Most of us use our heads too much to guide us. When we allow God to be the pilot of our own wings, not only can we fly, but we can also help others fly according to the spiritual air current that God provides them as well.

When we envelop ourselves in our tallitot, let us be reminded that our covenant and connection to God through the mitzvot enable us to sprout our wings of the שְׁכִינָה (*Shekhinah*) and soar close to God.

The Tallit in Poetry

Gods Change,
Prayers are Here to Stay
Yehuda Amichai

Whoever put on a tallis when he was young will never forget:
taking it out of the soft velvet bag, opening the folded shawl,
spreading it out, kissing the length of the neckband (embroidered
or trimmed in gold). Then swinging it in a great swoop overhead
like a sky, a wedding canopy, a parachute. And then winding it
around his head as in hide-and-seek, wrapping
his whole body in it, close and slow, snuggling into it like the cocoon
of a butterfly, then opening would-be wings to fly.
And why is the tallis striped and not checkered black-and-white
like a chessboard? Because squares are finite and hopeless.
Stripes come from infinity and to infinity they go
like airport runways where angels land and take off.
Whoever has put on a tallis will never forget.
When he comes out of a swimming pool or the sea,
he wraps himself in a large towel, spreads it out again
over his head, and again snuggles into it close and slow,
still shivering a little, and he laughs and blesses.

Jerusalem in Snow
Anat Bental

While velvet covers the town
Like a tallit,
The canopy of clouds
Like a wedding canopy above a bride
Dressed in white.
The wind ascends

With the sound and
melody
Of crystal,
The fragile heart
Like a flake of snow.

Jerusalem
Is like this snow,
Beautiful at moments,
But muddy for hours and days
When it melts.

Tallis: A Poem
Abraham Kinstlinger

My lips kiss the tsitsis during Sh'ma,
of your tallis which I have begun to wear
every Shabbos. The small one covering just
the shoulders, that (I think) you brought
from Germany.
Skimpy, in a way, incomplete, as
I have been since the day you died.
I was perhaps fourteen when I learned
to wind and knot the tsitsis, and
I replaced the tattered ones on this tallis,
tying tiny knots at each strand's end
to prevent it from unravelling.
You told me how good it felt for
you to wear the tallis whose
tsitsis I had made; and I was warmed.
Having inherited from you far more
than a piece of cloth, however hallowed ~
the shape of elongated fingers, nails,
thin legs, height,
the sunburst rays of temple lines ~
Slivered pangs of memory burst each time
Our lips kiss the tsitsis during Sh'ma.

My Tallit
Ruth Brin

You took me to your synagogue
for the first time on Yom Kippur, 1941.

Everything was white: the Torah mantles,
the rabbi's robes, the flowers.

White light fell on the white heads
and white shawl-covered shoulders of the men.

Everything was white
except for the dark dresses and black hats
we women were wearing.

You made me a talit,
you tied the knots, put it on my shoulders,
kissed me.

Now when we go to our synagogue
I am part of the whiteness,
part of the silent prayer for purity.

The Tallit in History

Garments of Prayer
Reuven Hammer

Words and music are the basic ways we use to express our devotion to God. There are, however, nonverbal means of communication that can be no less meaningful or important. The times when we sit or stand, the reclining of the head in sorrow or contrition, the bending of the knees, the steps backward we take when concluding the Amidah are all bodily symbols of emotions or ideas. Objects can also be part of worship. The lulav, etrog, and shofar are integral parts of prayer. The mezuzah on the doorpost is a declaration no less meaningful for being silent and static.

Garments are also an integral part of our approach to God. The descriptions of the clothing worn by the priests who officiated in the Temple and especially the garb of the High Priest, which included such items as a breastplate with twelve precious stones representing the twelve tribes and a golden plate worn on the forehead with the words "Holy to the Lord" cut out of it, are elaborately detailed in Exodus 28:6-43 and 39:2-31. What was important for the priests is also important for the individual Jew. The entire people of Israel is considered "a kingdom of priests and a holy nation" (Exod. 19:6), and this is expressed both through our high standards of ethics and morality and through ritual actions and garments. These garments are in themselves statements concerning our relationship with God:

> *Beloved are Israel, for the Holy One has surrounded*
> *them with mitzvot ~ tefillin on their heads and tefillin*
> *on their arms, [four] tzitzit on their garments, mezuzot*
> *on their doorways. Concerning them, David said: I*
> *praise You seven times each day for Your just rules* (Ps.
> 119:164).[1]

In Judaism today, the concept that all Jews are holy and the democratic basis of the synagogue have resulted in the fact that, unlike the Temple, special garments are not required by those who lead services in synagogues, while the ordinary Jew at prayer, no matter where, does use special garments. In the Temple, the officiants were clearly differentiated from the populace; in the synagogue, there is no differentiation and all are equally privileged to wear special garments. The use of special rabbinical robes, which was common in Europe even among Orthodox rabbis, was a practice borrowed from non-Jews in order to clearly demonstrate the status of "Jewish clergy."

In their origins, both the special garments of prayer were intended not merely for times of prayer but as part of the daily costume. The tallit and the tefillin, as well as the head covering (kippa) which is of much less importance in Jewish law, were to be worn the entire day. Thus Abraham Ibn Ezra, the medieval Spanish commentator, indicated that the wearing of the tzitzit (fringes), the main component of the tallit, was more important when not praying, since during prayer one was unlikely to be tempted to sin.[2]

Temptation occurs during the course of our everyday life, and it is then that we need to be reminded of our obligations to God. Although there are some who wear tzitzit in the form of an undergarment called arba kanfot ("four corners") or tallit katan (a small tallit) at all times, both the tallit and the tefillin have come to be thought of as appurtenances of prayer and are identified with the act of worship.

Covering the head is mentioned first in the rabbinic writings, where its use is an act of piety which seems to have been confined to the Sages and was not common usage.[3] Although it later became customary to cover one's head when praying or reading sacred texts, and among some to do so at all times, this has never been considered a "mitzvah" in the technical sense. While there are blessings to be recited when putting on a tallit or tefillin, there is no such blessing for donning a head covering. It has become, however, both a distinctive sign of Judaism and a symbol of modesty and humility.

Both the tzitzit and the tefillin can be traced back to the Bible. In the case of tefillin, we cannot be certain that the verses in the Torah that we identify as describing them were meant to be taken literally. Even if they did refer to some specific object, we do not know that those used during the biblical period were similar to the tefillin of later times. The tzitzit, however, are quite definitely of biblical origin. The commandment is found in a paragraph that became the third section of the Shema:

> *Speak to the Israelite people and instruct them to make for themselves fringes on the corners of their garments throughout the generations; let them attach a cord of blue to the fringe at each corner. That shall be your fringe; look at it and recall all the commandments of the Lord and observe them, so that you do not follow your heart and eyes in your lustful urge. Thus you shall be reminded to observe all My commandments and to be holy to your God (Num. 15:38-40).*

The description here is obviously of actual garments, and we are told exactly how these fringes were to be made. We are also given clear reasons for doing so: to keep us faithful to God and His commandments, and

to help us remember that we have been commanded
to be holy.

The biblical scholar Jacob Milgrom has shown that
this practice was based on the custom in the ancient
Near East of using elaborately decorated hems of
garments as signs of status.[4] The more important the
individual, the more elaborate the hem. Deep blue or
purple dye was expensive, being derived from the
murex snail and requiring large quantities of snails
for a small amount of dye. It was associated therefore
with nobility, and adding blue thread to the fringe
signified the worth and status of those who wore it.
The dye was also used in priestly garments (Exod. 28:6)
and in the inner curtain of the sanctuary (Exod. 26:1).
Thus the wearer was elevated to a status similar to
that of priesthood: holiness and nobility. Garments
with such fringes were a visible sign of the status that
Rabbi Akiva later characterized so astutely when he
said, "Beloved are the people of Israel, for they are
called the children of God."[5] Rabbinic Judaism also
connected the color to God:

> *Rabbi Meir said: Why is blue [tekhelet] different from all
> other colors? Because blue resembles the sea, the sea
> resembles the sky, and the sky resembles the throne of
> glory, as it is said, "Under His feet there was the
> likeness of a pavement of sapphire" (Exod. 24:10).*[6]

Rabbi Meir even went so far as to say that since the
verse that commands the fringes says, "Look at it"

(Num. 15:39), in the singular, rather than, "Look at them," it indicates that when one fulfills this commandment it is as if one were granted a glimpse of God Himself.[7]

In early biblical days there was no special garment such as the tallit of today. Rather, the garments worn by Israelites were made with a fringe in each place where the hem came to an end, and a blue thread was incorporated into the trim bordering the hem. In this way the Israelite was designated as part of God's noble and holy retinue. This was an outward sign of Israel's designation as a kingdom of priests, intended not so much so that others would recognize their position, but so that they themselves would be conscious of who they were and would not ignore the covenant made with God.

During the period of the Second Temple, the form of the tzitzit seems to have changed. Fringes were attached to any garment that had only four corners. Specific regulations came into existence as to how the white threads should be inserted or attached to the garment, together with a blue thread, but even then this was part of the normal garment rather than a special one. In addition, the way in which the thread was to be wound took on special significance. Each corner has one long thread and three short ones, folded to make eight threads. Since there are 613 commandments, the twists and knots are designed in such a way that, taken together with the numerical value of the word *tzitzit* itself (600), they add up to 613. Thus the very form of the fringes reminds one of the obligation to observe the commandments.

We also know for certain that women as well as men put such fringes on their garments. Rabbi Judah put fringes on the garments worn by all the women of his household.

> *The Sages taught: All are obligated to observe the mitzvah of tzitzit: priests, Levites, and Israelites, converts, women, and slaves.*[8]

Rabbi Simeon disagreed, believing that since they are worn only during the day, they fall into the category of commandments that are time-connected, and women are exempt from such commandments.[9] The Sages had ruled that since the Torah mentions that the tzitzit should be seen, they are to be worn only in the daytime. Night is not a time when things are visible. The only exception to this is the eve of Yom Kippur, Kol Nidre, when the extraordinary holiness and uniqueness of the occasion calls for the wearing of this symbol of holiness. Gradually the wearing of tzitzit became a male practice, although it was never actually forbidden to women. Today, the practice of women wearing a tallit is becoming more common outside of Orthodox circles.

A rabbinic tale, based on the biblical wording that the fringes are to help us curb our "lustful urges," illustrates the way in which the Sages thought the tzitzit were to assist us. A student spent a fortune to go to a world-renowned harlot. She had prepared seven beds, one on top of another, six of silver and the seventh of gold. She awaited him on the golden bed, and as he climbed up to reach it the four tzitzit of his garment hit him across the face, whereupon he shamefacedly lowered himself and sat down on the ground. When she asked him what was wrong, he explained that the tzitzit were witnesses which had reminded him of his obligations and his wrongdoing. The woman was so impressed, the story goes on, that she sought out the academy he was attending, studied Judaism, converted, and married the student.[10]

Eventually a garment developed, resembling a cloak, that is worn over regular clothing when prayers are recited. The fringes and not the garment itself are the essence of the commandment. The blessing recited when putting it on makes it clear that the commandment being fulfilled is the one the Torah mentions: wearing fringes. It is: "Blessed are You, O Lord our God, king of the universe, who has sanctified us by His commandments and commanded us to wrap ourselves in tzitzit."

---

[1]Menachot 43b.

[2] See Ibn Ezra to Numbers 15:39.

---

3 Shabbat 118b. Rav Huna considered it a mark of his piety, deserving reward, that he "never walked four cubits bareheaded." See also Shabbat 156b.

4 See Jacob Milgrom, *The JPS Torah Commentary: Numbers* (Philadelphia, 1990), pp. 410ff. The Torah places the section concerning the fringes after the story of the spies. The spies fell victim to "scouting" after their own eyes (Num. 13:17, 13:21, 13:32). The fringes are intended to prevent one from following ("scouting after" ~ the Hebrew is the same) one's eyes and heart, and thus going astray, as did the spies and the Israelites who followed them (Num. 15:39).

5 Avot 3:18.

6 Menachot 43b; Sifre Numbers 115.

7 Sifre Numbers 115.

8 Menachot 43a.

9 Ibid; Sifre Numbers 115.

10 Menachot 44a; Sifre Numbers 115.

In Search of Lost Hilazon
Mordecai Kornfeld

Royal colors

> *The People of Israel shall wear on the tzitzit of the corners [ritual strings that hang from the corners of four-cornered garments] a string of tekhelet [wool dyed with a certain blue dye]* (Bamidbar 15:38).

> *Tekhelet is only kosher if it is made from the hilazon; if it is not made from the hilazon it is invalid* (Tosefta Menachot 9:6, Beraita in Massechet Tzitzit 1:10).

The תְּכֵלֶת (*tekhelet*) ~ or Biblical blue ~ dye is mentioned dozens of times throughout the Tanakh, usually together with another dye named argaman (Royal, or Tyrian, purple). In the ancient world, these two dyes were extremely valuable ~ they were worth many times their weight in gold. Clothing dyed with these pigments was generally reserved for royalty, or at least for high-ranking nobles. Tekhelet and argaman were also used for dyeing the priestly garments worn by the Kohanim in the Holy Temple. In Parashat Sh'lah, the Torah gives every Jew the right ~ even the obligation ~ to wear a string of this royal tekhelet on his garments. Perhaps the inclusion of tekhelet in our צִיצָת (*tzitzit*) was also meant to demonstrate the idea expressed in the Mishnah:

> *"All the Bnai Yisroel are like sons of kings"*
> (Shabbat 111a).

The Midrash puts it even more succinctly:

> *The tekhelet reminds us of the dominion of Hashem Himself. It is attached to our garments to show all that we are none other than His own children* (Socher Tov Tehillim 90, "V'Hadarcha Al B'neihem").

Throughout the times of the Mishnah and the Talmud, the tekhelet string was included in the tzitziot of the men of Israel. Even the later Amora'im [sages of the Gemara] who lived in Babylonia ~ far from the Mediterranean coast, where the tekhelet was produced ~ had tekhelet (Menachot 43a, Sanhedrin 12a). Unfortunately, at some point after this time, the art of the manufacture of tekhelet was lost, and its use discontinued. This is already apparent in the later Midrashim (Bemidbar Rabba 17:5; Tanchuma, end of Sh'lah), which mention that the tekhelet has been "hidden away" (*nignaz*). It is conjectured that the production of tekhelet ceased some time in the seventh or eighth century, perhaps as a result of the devastation and upheaval caused by the Arab conquest of Eretz Israel in 683.

What exactly is this hilazon from which the tekhelet dye is extracted? Where has it been "hidden" all these years? Is it possible to reconstruct the long-lost art of tekhelet production? What is the nature of the tekhelet that some men wear today on their צִיצַת (*tzitzit*) ~ is it authentic or just an artificial substitute for the real thing? Let us take an excursion into the world of the hilazon and the tekhelet dye and see if we can unravel some of the mystery that pervades this fascinating subject.

Before we start, it must be pointed out that in the field of tekhelet research a great debt of gratitude is due to the former chief Rabbi of Ireland and later of Israel, Rav Yitzchak Isaac Herzog, who did a major study on the topic at the age of 24 for his doctoral thesis. In it, he combined his exceptional scholarship in 8 different disciplines and 12 languages, not to mention a tremendous erudition in Judaic sources. To this day, his thesis remains *the* authoritative work on the subject, from both a scholarly and a Talmudic standpoint. The thesis was written in English in 1920. It was later adapted into a Hebrew version by the author, which was published in installments in the periodical *HaHed* from 1932 to 1935. The Hebrew version was recently reprinted in full in the book *Hatekhelet*, by Rav Menachem Burstein (Jerusalem, 1988), pp. 352-437. The longer English version was printed in Israel in *The Royal Purple and the Biblical Blue*, edited by Ehud Spanier (Keter, 1987).

Fins and Scales?

What color is the tekhelet dye? Here we have very clear, specific information. The Gemara in Bava Metzia 61b says that the color of tekhelet is indistinguishable from that of indigo ("Kala Ilan"- see Sefer Ha'Aruch). When it comes to the hilazon, though, the information we are given is much more sketchy.

From where does the hilazon, the source of the tekhelet dye, come? In Ezekiel 27:7, we read that the most professional production sites of tekhelet were to be found in "the islands of Elishah," which have been identified as either Italy (see Targum, ibid.) or Cyprus. The Talmud tells us in several places that the only place tekhelet was to be found in Eretz Yisrael was in the territory of the tribe of Zevulun, which was along the Mediterranean coast from Haifa and northward to Tyre (Shabbat 26a, Megilla 6a).

Let us turn now to the identity of the hilazon itself. What sort of creature is it? The only explicit source about this question is the following:

> *"The body of the hilazon resembles the sea* [alternate reading: resembles the sky - MK], *and its body is similar to that of a fish. It comes up once every seventy* [alternate reading: seven - MK] *years.*

[This may be an exaggeration employed to emphasize the scarcity of the species - MK.] *The tekhelet dye is obtained from its blood [secretion], and it is therefore very expensive"* (Menachot 44a; Beraita in Masechet Tzitzit).

Another hint to the nature of the hilazon is given in Shabbat 74b, where we are told that the hilazon was gathered from the sea in nets.

Tosafot (to Shabbat 73b "Mefarek," 75a "Hatzad"), apparently basing his words on the above Gemara in Shabbat, intimates that the hilazon is a type of fish, which squirms around in the net after it is caught. A similar view is expressed by Rabbeinu Bachya in the beginning of Parashat Terumah (25:3), where the Torah mentions three dyes used in the construction of the Mishkan (the movable Tabernacle of the desert) ~ tekhelet, argaman and *tola'at shani*. The last of these three dyes is generally understood to mean "scarlet from a worm." Rabbeinu Bachya asks how this is possible, since the Gemara (Shabbat 28b) says that only products that are kosher to be eaten were used in the Mishkan, and worms ~ or their secretions - are not kosher! He therefore explains that the scarlet dye in question was not actually taken from worms, but from some sort of berry that *contained* the worms. Following this approach, it may be concluded that the hilazon, which is a sea creature, must be a regular fish, with fins and scales, for these are the only kosher sea creatures.

The approach of Rabbeinu Bachya, however, is quite difficult. It seems clear from the Talmud Yerushalmi (Kilayim 9:1), and it is also a known fact, that the scarlet dye of tola'at shani was indeed extracted from a worm (the female *Kermococcus Vermilis*, an insect that breeds on a certain species of oak) and not from a berry. Rabbeinu Bachya's words are therefore very hard to accept; a copyist's error in the piece cannot be discounted. As far as how a non-kosher creature could be used in the manufacture of an item for use in the Mishkan, we must say that it is only the actual *materials* used in the Mishkan that were subject to this rule, not the dyes. The pigments, which are not tangible objects in the finished product, were not included in this prohibition. If this is so, we are not bound to assume that the hilazon was any more a kosher creature than the shani worm.

Squids and Snails

So if the hilazon may not have been a kosher fish, then what kind of fish was it?

In the late 19th century, a talmudic researcher by the name of Yehudah Levisohn wrote in his work *Talmudic Zoology* (p. 284-5) that the hilazon was a type of squid known as the cuttlefish. Levisohn based his conclusion on an inference from a statement of the Rambam in *Hilchot Tzitzit* 2:2. Shortly afterwards, a brilliant Hassidic Rebbe, Rav Gershon Henoch Leiner of Radzin, came to the same conclusion. He carried the conclusion one step further, though, actually developing a process whereby the sepia (inky secretion) of the cuttlefish, which normally produces a dark brown dye, was transformed into a blue dye! The dye turned out to be identical, chemically, to a common synthetic light-blue dye invented in 1704, known as Prussian blue. The Radziner Rebbe authored three large volumes to support his thesis, purporting to prove that he had rediscovered the long-lost tekhelet, and set up a factory where the dye was produced. His followers adopted his opinion and began wearing the new tekhelet string in their צִיצִת (*tzitzit*). With the exception of the Breslover Hasidim, however, the innovation was not accepted by the rest of the Jewish world, and his movement was even met with a substantial amount of opposition.

It is interesting to note that the method used by the Radziner Rebbe to produce tekhelet consisted of boiling the sepia, iron filings, and potash together at tremendously high temperatures to produce the pigment ferric ferrocyanide. Dye chemists are quick to point out, however, that this process doesn't make any unique use of the squid's inky secretion. In fact, the sepia itself disintegrates and never makes it to the final product, leaving behind only its nitrogen atoms. Any nitrogen-containing compound will produce the same result, if substituted for the squid ink! In fact, a similar process is used by any organic chemistry student as a test for nitrogen in compounds. (I thank the chemist Dr. Israel Ziderman of the Jerusalem Fiber

Institute, founder of the Tekhelet Foundation, for giving me of his time to clarify this point. See also *Hatekhelet*, pp. 413-6, for the results Rav Herzog obtained upon submitting the Radziner Rebbe's tekhelet to chemical analysis.)

Unfortunately, there are a number of technical difficulties with the tekhelet produced according to the Radziner method. Firstly, tekhelet was known to be absolutely indelible (Menachot 43b), while the Radziner tekhelet can fade (a process called "bleeding") when scrubbed with common detergents (see *Hatekhelet* p. 179). Secondly, the blue color that he produced wasn't the blue shade of indigo, but rather a more metallic blue (see *Hatekhelet* p. 413). Also, the squid he used is of a species that is relatively common in the Mediterranean Sea, and this does not correspond to the statements made about the rarity of the hilazon (*Hatekhelet* p. 177). Furthermore, there are no more squids in the land of Zevulun than anywhere else in the Mediterranean. The only place they can be found in particular abundance is in the area of Italy (*Hatekhelet* p. 178)!

Perhaps the strongest objection to the Radziner tekhelet, though, is that the word *hilazon* is used in numerous places in Hazal (rabbinic sources) as a general term, meaning "snail." In Shir HaShirim Rabbah (4:11), a hilazon is a creature that lives inside a shell. (See the Radziner Rebbe's words on this matter in *Hatekhelet*, p. 174. His explanation is not very satisfying). Also, in

Bechorot (Mishna 6:2) and in Kelim (12:1) something with a spiral or twisted appearance is dubbed *hilazon*. In Sanhedrin 91a, we are told that hilazons appear on the ground after a rain. It seems clear from all these sources that hilazon is being used in the context of "snail," and it is therefore logical to assume that the famous hilazon that produces tekhelet is a particular kind of snail. Rashi (Sanhedrin 91a) indeed tells us that the hilazon creature is a type of slug, which definitely allows for the possibility of it being a mollusk. The Gemara in Menachot was actually careful to point out that the hilazon is *"similar* to a fish," i.e. a fish-like sea creature. It is not a fish itself.

The identification of the hilazon as a type of snail enables us to solve another puzzle. Tosafot in Shabbat 75a (*"HaTzad"*) quotes a statement from Talmud Yerushalmi to the effect that catching a hilazon on the Shabbat does not constitute a violation of the prohibition against trapping or catching animals on Shabbat. Tosafot is at a loss to explain why a hilazon should be an exception to the rule. Now that we have identified the hilazon as a type of snail, however, the answer is obvious. There is a rule that if an animal cannot easily escape (if it is blind or wounded, etc.) then "catching" that animal does not constitute a violation of the prohibition of trapping on Shabbat (Shabbat 106b). Certainly a snail cannot move away easily from its trapper! It is true that the Talmud Bavli asserts that the prohibition against trapping is violated by one who traps a hilazon. This should not be taken as evidence that the hilazon is not a snail. The Talmud Bavli may agree to the Yerushalmi's identification of the hilazon, but nevertheless prohibit its capture on other grounds. Perhaps picking out the barely discernible hilazon on the sea bed cannot be compared to ensnaring a prominent helpless creature above the ground.

What of the fact that the Gemara says that hilazons are harvested with a net? Doesn't this seem to imply that they are a type of fish? The answer to this may lie in the fact that even today snails are captured by spreading baited nets (they are considered a delicacy in many countries). The bait lures the snails into the nets, which are then raised. Alternatively, the nets may have been used to confine the already harvested snails in a saltwater environment, until the dye could be made from them. (The Gemara tells us in Shabbat 75a that if the hilazon is allowed to die before its juice is extracted, it cannot be made into a suitable dye.)

Argaman and Tekhelet

But which of the many species of snails is the one that produces the tekhelet dye?

It was pointed out earlier that tekhelet is often mentioned in conjunction with argaman. (In fact, in the Talmudic literature, the term תְּכֵלֶת - *tekhelet* is often used to refer to either of the two.) In the middle 17th century, an English naturalist named Thomas

Geig wrote that he found a snail containing within it a liquid that becomes a purplish dye after being extracted from the snail and exposed to sunlight. At around the same time, someone named Saul Bochart *(Hierozoicon,* 1663) proved from ancient sources that argaman was produced from snails. Shortly afterwards, researchers put the two facts together, concluding that Geig's snail was indeed the source used by the ancients to produce argaman *(Hatekhelet,* pp. 252, 371, 418).

In fact, archaeologists have uncovered numerous ancient dye-producing factories all over the Mediterranean coast (mostly in the northeastern area, "from Haifa to Tyre"), with large heaps of snail shells alongside them. These shells have been identified as belonging to three distinct species of snails: *Purpura Haemastoma, Murex Brandaris* and *Murex Trunculus*. That these snails were the source of Tyrian purple ~ argaman ~ has become accepted as a historical fact.

These snails are in fact much more numerous along the northern coast of Eretz Yisroel than along the southern coast, with their population steadily increasing as one goes north. South of Haifa, the snails are few and far between. This corresponds nicely with the description of the hilazon's distribution that is presented by Hazal.

The identities of these snails were well-known to Rav Herzog when he wrote his work on the topic of tekhelet. And, as he himself pointed out, it seems clear from several Biblical and historical sources that the Jews and the gentiles extracted their blue dyes from the same creature (*Hatekhelet* pp. 426-7. See also Shabbat 26a, and Rashi ad loc. *"U'Lyogvim"*). Nevertheless, he rejected the idea that one or all of these species may be the true tekhelet hilazon for several reasons. First of all, the color of their shells is white, which contradicts the Gemara's description (quoted above) that the hilazon's body "resembles the sea," i.e., is of a bluish hue. Furthermore, and more importantly, the dye extracted from these creatures is purple in color, and not indigo. The above-mentioned snails were clearly the source of argaman, or *purpura* in Latin. However, tekhelet, referred to in Latin by Josephus and Philo as *hyakinthos*, may have been produced from another snail altogether!

Rav Herzog's Tekhelet

R. Herzog suggested that there was indeed another snail, distinct from the above-mentioned snails, from which tekhelet was derived. The snail he chose is known as *Janthina Pallida Harvey*. It is found in the Mediterranean, and has a beautiful violet-blue shell. When excited, it discharges a secretion of the same color. It is quite rare, and lives in colonies that have population explosions every four to seven years, when large numbers of them are washed ashore! All the pieces of the puzzle seem to fit now (*Hatekhelet*, p.427)! Over the last two years, serious research has been done to determine whether a blue dye can indeed be

made from the Janthina's secretion. So far, the efforts
have not met with much success. The secretion can
produce a reddish-bluish color on a fabric, but within
a matter of hours the color turns black. Aside from
that, the dye washes right out of the fabric when
brought into contact with water. In fact, the most
advanced modern testing has not been able to even
dissolve the secretion in any chemical solution ~ the
most basic requirement of any known dye. Instead of
dissolving in liquid, the Janthina's ink forms a
suspension. In this state, it cannot be induced to bind
to a fabric. More research into the chemical makeup of
the secretion is still necessary.

Aside from this technical difficulty, there are several
problems with identifying the hilazon as the Janthina
snail. For one thing, as with the cuttlefish, it is no
more common along the shore of Zevulun than
anywhere else in the Mediterranean. For another, as
Rav Herzog himself points out, no Janthina shells
have ever been discovered in any archaeological site,
nor is it mentioned anywhere in the Greek or Roman
literature that discuss blue dye. It thus appears not to
have been in use in the ancient world.

Modern Tekhelet

A contemporary of Rav Herzog, Alexander Dedekind
of Vienna, suggested in his work *Archeological Zoology*
(Vienna, 1898, p. 467) that the blue dye of tekhelet actually
did come from the snails found near the ancient dye

vats. He differentiated between the tekhelet and the argaman snails, singling out *Murex Trunculus* (known in modern Hebrew as *Argemon Keheh Kotzim*, or "short spiked Purpura") as the source of the blue tekhelet. In contrast, the other two species were used exclusively for the production of argaman. He bases this assumption on the fact that not far from Sidon, an ancient dyeing site was discovered that had near it two separate piles of shells. In one pile, the shells of *Purpura Haemastoma* and *Murex Brandaris* were mixed together, while in the other only shells of *Murex Trunculus* were found (*Hatekhelet,* p. 421). This certainly seems to support the idea that *Murex Trunculus* was used for a different purpose than the other two snails. In fact, *M. Trunculus* produces a slightly bluer dye than the other two. Although he personally favored his *Janthina* theory, Rav Herzog himself reluctantly admitted that "the logical conclusion would certainly appear to be that the blue pigment produced by the hilazon was obtained using the *Murex Trunculus* dye... it is highly unlikely that the tekhelet hilazon was not the *Murex Trunculus*" (*Hatekhelet,* p. 421). The evidence seems to point overwhelmingly to *Murex Trunculus* as being the source of tekhelet.

Is there a way that Rav Herzog's objections to identifying *Murex Trunculus* as the hilazon can be overcome? The first objection can be answered easily. Rav Herzog pointed out that the shells of *Murex Trunculus* were white and not "similar to the sea." However, his conclusion was based on the color of the centuries-old shells found by the archaeologists or of museum samples. As a matter of fact, though, when the snail is first removed from the sea, it does indeed have a bluish-purple tinge to it, produced by sea-fouling. (As I gaze at the *Murex* shell that is presently on my desk, I can still see on it a pronounced purplish-bluish tint.)

The other problem raised was that the secretion of *Murex Trunculus* turns purple and not blue. Rav Herzog himself raised the possibility that "there might have been some scheme known to the ancients for obtaining a blue dye out of this secretion" (*Hatekhelet* p. 423). Sure enough, recent research has shown that when the secretion is exposed to bright sunlight immediately upon being extracted from the snail, the sunlight breaks down a certain chemical bond in the liquid and it subsequently forms a blue dye. In fact, the resulting dye consists mostly of components bearing the exact same chemical makeup as indigo! Although this is true of all three of the snails mentioned before, *Murex Trunculus* yields this blue color much more readily than the others. *M. Trunculus* does not require a lengthy exposure to the sun in order for the chemical reactions to take place. (Credit for this discovery goes to the late Otto Elsner of the Shenkar Institute of Fibers in Ramat Gan, Israel, whose words can be found in *Hatekhelet*, pp. 299-302; see also p. 423, note 39).

All the difficulties seem to have been adequately dealt with ~ except for one. What is the once-in-seven(ty)-years cycle of "coming up" (*oleh echad l'shiv'im shana*) mentioned by the Gemara? Does the *Murex Trunculus* snail show any unusual prominence every seventy (or seven) years? So far, no such behavior has been determined in the *Murex*. It should be pointed out, however, that much of the headway made in hilazon research is quite recent, and there has not yet been sufficient opportunity to study the nature of the *Murex* snail. We may yet discover that there is indeed some sort of regular periodical occurrence involved in *Murex*'s life cycle. It is interesting to note that a few kilometers north of Haifa there is a ravine known to the Arabs as Wadi Hilzun, which is near a mountain called Mount Hilazon. Rashi (Megilla 6a, Sanhedrin 91a; see also Rashi Menachot 44a) explains the "coming up" of the hilazon as the hilazon emerging from the sea and ascending the mountains. Is it possible that every few years (or decades) there is some sort of mass migration of these snails through Wadi Hilzun and up Mount Hilazon, from which these places may have been given their names in ancient times? Only time will tell!

The Tekhelet Team

In the practical realm, we must acknowledge the work of a scholar in Jerusalem, Harav Eliyahu Tevger (author of *Kelil Tekhelet*). Although faced with great technical difficulties and high costs, he undertook the

202 / Enveloped in Light

project of locating and collecting enough of the *M. Trunculus* snails, mastering the technique of turning their secretion into a high-quality blue dye, and applying the dye to wool ~ all this despite the general antipathy of the scientific community and of the Society for the Preservation of Nature in Israel. Eight years ago, his initiative first saw success, and he used his product to dye wool threads according to the requirements of the Halacha. These were made into tekhelet for צִיצָת (*tzitzit*) for the first time in fifteen centuries! Along with three others who have dedicated themselves to this endeavor ~ Joel Guberman, Ari Greenspan and Baruch Sterman ~ Rav Tevger has formed the *P'til Tekhelet* Society. Just two years ago, they started to mass-produce their tekhelet, using thousands of snails imported from various countries on the Northern Mediterranean coast that consider the snail a delicacy. At the time of this writing (June 5755), they are in the final stages of dyeing their second 300-string batch, and already have many more orders than they can handle. Working on this project during their free time, the group is offering the tekhelet to the public for cost-price; $50 a set.

So now what?

In Conclusion

What does all this mean for us? Can it be said halachically that the true tekhelet ~ or at least a very likely candidate for it ~ has been rediscovered? Is it now binding upon us once again, as it was in antiquity, to add this dye to our צִיצִת (*tzitzit*)?

Halachically, there does not yet seem to be an obligation to wear the present tekhelet. True, there is a rule that "when there is a doubt as to the correct halachic ruling, one must follow the more stringent view when it comes to a question of a Torah (as opposed to Rabbinical) precept." This would seem to imply that even if our identification of hilazon with *Murex Trunculus* is not absolutely certain, we should be obligated to wear the newly discovered tekhelet just in case. Nevertheless, due to various considerations that are not within the scope of this article, that ruling would not seem to apply in this case.

However, there is another interesting ramification of the emergence of the tekhelet. Rav Chaim Vital in *Shaar HaKavvanot* (Tzitzit, Drush 4) writes that tekhelet represents Hashem's presence being clearly felt by all. This is why, he tells us, tekhelet was only widely accessible during, or close to, the times when the Temple was standing. These were the times when Hashem's Presence among Israel was manifest for all to see. After the exile and its attendant hardships intensified, however, when Hashem's Presence among His people became less evident, tekhelet became "hidden" as well. If so, the return of tekhelet may be taken as an indication that the manifestation of Hashem's Presence in this world, too, will be returning to its former state. (There is also a tradition from Rav Nachman of Breslov that, some time before the advent of the Messianic era, the mitzvah of tekhelet will be reinstated ~ see *Hatekhelet* p. 186, note 21; see also *Likutei Tfilot* 1:49.) Some Rabbinic authorities even showed reluctance to acknowledge the halachic validity of the various tekhelets because of these far-reaching implications.

Whatever hidden meaning there may be in the almost mystical reappearance of the hilazon and the tekhelet during the past decades, may we merit to actually see Hashem's hand in the final redemption, speedily in our days!

In Search of Holy Snail
Ari Z. Zivotofsky

The traditional prayer shawl, customarily adorned with white threads dangling from each corner, has been sprouting a new color on its corners. The story behind this begins in the Bible, continues through the Talmudic period, makes a big comeback in the early part of the 20th century, and is continuing to be played out in modern chemistry labs and yeshivot today. First, the background.

One of the most familiar ritual garments, one that is found in virtually every synagogue, is the tallit (ritual prayer shawl). It originated as a four-cornered cloak worn in ancient times, on which צִיצָת (*tzitzit*) ~ ritual fringes ~ were attached to each corner.

The tallit's origins are found in the Book of Numbers in a section customarily recited twice daily as part of the Sh'ma. There, the Jews are commanded to attach fringes on all four-cornered garments, not only those designated for prayer, as a reminder of G-d's presence. When the four-cornered cloak gave way to other garb, Jewish men began wearing a "mini-tallit," known as אַרְבַּע כַּנְפוֹת (*arba kanfot*) ~ four corners, or טַלִּית קָטָן (*tallit katan*) ~ small tallit, under their shirts all day. Additionally, we are all familiar with the large tallit worn during all morning services (except on Tisha B'Av) and at the Yom Kippur evening service.

The material portion of the tallit has very few religious dictates. It is usually a large woolen rectangle, traditionally white with black or blue "racing" stripes across the front and back. This design was the impetus for the modern Israeli flag. In recent years, some have taken to designing multicolored, "modern" tallitot. Jewish law has little objection to this as long as the tallit is large enough to be deemed a garment, has the צִיצָת (*tzitzit*) properly attached, and, preferably, is wool.

The one area that is usually not tampered with, however, is the strings, the actual צִיצָת (*tzitzit*). They are white on almost all modern tallitot. But it has not always been that way. The Bible actually requires that one thread (or, according to others, two threads) on each corner be תְּכֵלֶת (*tekhelet*), a special shade of blue that was made from a sea creature known as a hilazon. This blue string was considered the principal feature of the צִיצָת (*tzitzit*). A highly prized dye, literally worth its weight in gold, תְּכֵלֶת (*tekhelet*) was scarce even in ancient times, and was used by royalty.

During the Talmudic period, the Romans issued edicts against the Jewish תְּכֵלֶת (*tekhelet*) industry, forcing it underground. Following the Arab conquest of Palestine, the secret of how to make תְּכֵלֶת (*tekhelet*) was effectively lost and, by the mid-eighth century, the fringes Jews wore on their garments were only white.

The story of the rediscovery of תְּכֵלֶת (*tekhelet*) is a puzzle full of intrigue, deception, deduction, and logic. The major players include archaeologists, marine biologists, chemists, sailors, the leader of a Hasidic sect, a former chief rabbi of Israel, and some good friends of mine in Israel ~ a physicist, a physical therapist, and a dentist. The first piece in the puzzle was a chance encounter in 1858. French zoologist Henri de Lacaze-Duthiers was on a scientific expedition when one of the fishermen on his boat took a snail, broke it open and smeared it on his shirt. The fisherman boasted that the yellow stain would soon change color in the sunlight and, when that happened, Lacaze-Duthiers immediately realized that the snail (of the *Murex Trunculus* species) was the long-lost source of some of the ancient dyes.

Unaware of Lacaze-Duthiers' findings, Rabbi Gershon Henoch Leiner, a Hasidic rebbe from the Russian-Polish town of Radzyn, published a pamphlet in 1887 announcing that he was to begin searching for the lost hilazon sea creature in an effort to bring back the תְּכֵלֶת (*tekhelet*) to the Jewish people. After studying marine specimens in an aquarium in Naples, Italy, and being tricked by a duplicitous chemist about the dyeing process, Rabbi Leiner set up a factory to produce a dye thought to be תְּכֵלֶת (*tekhelet*). He used the cuttlefish *Sepia ficinalis*, a type of squid, for his dye. Within two years, 10,000 of his followers, the Radzyner Hasidim, were wearing his תְּכֵלֶת (*tekhelet*).

Rabbi Leiner published two more books to counter the strong opposition encountered from other rabbis, but the split between his followers and others who would not wear his תְּכֵלֶת (*tekhelet*) ran deep, to the point that Radzyner Hasidim were often not allowed to be buried in regular Jewish cemeteries.

In 1913, then Chief Rabbi of Ireland (and later of Israel; also father of Chaim Herzog, who served as President of Israel) Isaac Herzog wrote a doctoral dissertation on the subject of Hebrew prophyrology ("the study of purple" ~ a word Herzog coined). He requested from the Radzyners a sample of their תְּכֵלֶת (*tekhelet*), as well as their detailed manufacturing process.

Much to Herzog's surprise, he found that the Radzyner תְּכֵלֶת (*tekhelet*) was no more than the popular organic dye known as Prussian blue, and thus likely not the true blue תְּכֵלֶת (*tekhelet*). Ironically, while discrediting the Radzyn תְּכֵלֶת (*tekhelet*), Herzog was responsible for saving their process for future generations. When survivors of Radzyn made their way to Israel after the Holocaust, it was Herzog who provided the information needed to reestablish their תְּכֵלֶת (*tekhelet*) industry, which flourishes in Israel to this day.

Meanwhile, Herzog was aware of strong evidence associating the *Murex Trunculus* snail with the sea creature, including the work of Lacaze-Duthiers. Among other things, he knew archaeologists in Tyre and elsewhere on the Mediterranean had uncovered mounds of *Murex* shells; thus he felt strongly that *Murex Trunculus* could be the hilazon. However, due to some unresolved questions, he did not conclusively identify the hilazon or begin manufacture of תְּכֵלֶת (*tekhelet*). He even proposed a possible alternative snail, *Janthina*, raising another set of questions.

Within the last few decades, many of Herzog's questions regarding *Murex Trunculus* have been addressed by a group of Israeli professors and rabbis, who have also worked out the details of the ancient process. Within the last ten years, an organization in Israel, the *Ptil Tekhelet* Foundation, was established in an effort to produce תְּכֵלֶת (*tekhelet*) and make it available to the general public.

This effort has included the participation of a number of my friends who go scuba diving in different cities on the Mediterranean for *Murex Trunculus*. There is strong evidence that it is the hilazon sea creature. A number of prominent rabbis have accepted the *Trunculus* snail as the long-lost hilazon, and צִיצַת (*tzitzit*) with possibly authentic תְּכֵלֶת (*tekhelet*) are now being worn, even by some men here in Cleveland, for the first time in more than 1,300 years.

The Tallit in Halakhah and Practice

The Tallit: A Halakhic Summary
Menachem Raab

The Source for Wearing a Tallit

The טַלִּית (*tallit*) is a garment worn by Jewish men during religious services. It is a four-cornered garment with special fringes, known as צִיצָת (*tzitzit*), attached to the four corners. The term צִיצָת (*tzitzit*) is Biblical and is found in the Book of Numbers (15:38-39).[1] The Lord tells Moses to instruct the Children of Israel "to make for themselves צִיצָת (*tzitzit*) ~ fringes ~ on the corners of their garments." They were instructed further to "attach a cord of תְּכֵלֶת (*tekhelet*)[2] (blue)" to the צִיצָת (*tzitzit*) at each corner. The reason the Torah gives for the precept of צִיצָת (*tzitzit*) is so that "you may look at it and recall all the commandments...."

Halakhah elucidates this law and requires that all garments that have four corners must have these צִיצָת (*tzitzit*) attached to the corners. The *Sefer Hahinukh*[3] expounds on this by saying that this mitzvah "requires that we insert צִיצִת (*tzitzit*) in a garment that we wear...and this obligation is incurred when the garment has four corners or more...and that the material be made from wool or flax." This source further comments that from Rabbinic teachings we learn that we do not insert צִיצִת (*tzitzit*) in garments of five or more corners.[4] Furthermore, it states that if we cannot acquire the necessary blue or the white threads, the mitzvah may be performed by using only the white or blue threads exclusively.

It seems that in Talmudic times the men wore a four-cornered garment wrapped around their bodies. This was known as a טַלִּית (*tallit*).[5] The garment had the צִיצִת (*tzitzit*) attached to its four corners. Since this was the normal garb at the time, the טַלִּית (*tallit*) was not necessarily associated with prayer and had no religious significance. We are told in the Talmud,[6] Rabbi Ashi said: I saw when there was trouble in the world, Rabbi Kahana would remove his cloak (*tallit*) and clasp his hands and pray and would say, "(I am) like a slave before his master." When there was peace, he would put it on, and would cover himself and would wrap himself and pray. We are also told in the same passage that judges would wrap themselves in the garment when sitting in judgment.[7]

Today, of course, we generally do not wear four-cornered garments. Hence, the mitzvah of צִיצִת (*tzitzit*) would fall into disuse and would be forgotten. Accordingly, the *Shulhan Arukh*[8] says that every individual should be careful to wear a טַלִּית קָטָן (*tallit katan*),[9] or a small tallit, all day so as to be mindful of the mitzvah at all times. He should at least wear a טַלִּית (*tallit*) during prayers. The *Zohar*[10] says that one who reads the *Sh'ma* without wearing a טַלִּית (*tallit*) is giving false testimony. This is so since in the *Sh'ma* we read the commandment to wear צִיצִת (*tzitzit*),[11] and the individual is reading it and not complying with its requirement.[12] In most cases, the טַלִּית (*tallit*) has a decoration of blue stripes, and some would like to explain that this is a semblance of the blue thread or תְּכֵלֶת (*tekhelet*) originally required by the Torah as part of the צִיצִת (*tzitzit*).[13] The stripes may be black or other colors, or there may be no stripes at all.

The Talmud discusses the permissibility of putting woolen צִיצִת (*tzitzit*) on a linen garment and vice versa.[14] The problem arises from the biblical prohibition of wearing garments made with threads of wool and linen woven together (Deut. 22:11). This is known as *shatnez* or *kil'ayim*. The conclusion of the Talmudic discussion is that it is permissible. This is based on a principle that states when we have a distinctive positive commandment that conflicts with a negative commandment, the positive one gets preference.[15] This principle is deduced from the juxtaposition of two passages in the Torah. The first tells us not to wear combined fibers, wool and linen together (Deut. 22:11). This verse is followed immediately by the commandment to place the צִיצִת

(*tzitzit*) on the four corners of our garments. Hence, the Sages learn that we are instructed to wear צִיצָת (*tzitzit*) even if the combination of the צִיצָת (*tzitzit*) and the garment results in transgressing the law of mixed fibers.[16] To avoid this problem entirely, traditionally, a woolen טַלִית (*tallit*) is worn. Some people will use a linen or silk טַלִית (*tallit*), though most traditionally-minded groups frown upon this practice.

The B'rakhah and When the Tallit is Worn

There is a difference in the בְּרָכָה (*b'rakhah*) made for the טַלִית (*tallit*) and that made for the טַלִית קָטָן (*tallit katan*).

For the former, one should recite the formula for a בְּרָכָה (*b'rakhah*) and conclude with the words לְהִתְעַטֵּף בַּצִיצָת (*lehitatef batzitzit*). For the latter, the wording ends with עַל מִצְוַת צִיצָת (*al mitzvat tzitzit*).

If one removes his טַלִית (*tallit*), even if he intended to put it on again soon, he has to recite the בְּרָכָה (*b'rakhah*) again. This is the position of the author of the *Shulhan Arukh*. The Rema, however, maintains that if, when removing the טַלִית (*tallit*) he intends to put it on again soon, he need not repeat the בְּרָכָה (*b'rakhah*).[17]

It is interesting to note that Ibn Ezra[18] writes that "in my opinion one is more obligated to wear צִיצָת

(*tzitzit*) at times other than during the time of prayer so that he remembers (the mitzvot) and he will not go astray nor transgress at all times, for during prayers he will not perform a transgression."

The Talmud[19] tells us that only day garments require צִיצָת (*tzitzit*). Night garments are exempt, based on the Torah passage that states "and you shall see it" (Num. 15:39). Normally, the nighttime is not considered a time when one can see the צִיצָת (*tzitzit*) without artificial lighting. Thus, one need not wear צִיצָת (*tzitzit*) at night. It is for this reason that a טַלִית (*tallit*) is not worn during the מַעֲרִיב (*Ma'ariv*) or night services.[20] Since this is, therefore, a mitzvah dependent on time, women are exempt from this precept,[21] and they do not wear a טַלִית (*tallit*) at any time.[22] The reason a טַלִית (*tallit*) is not worn during the מִנְחָה (*Minhah*) service is probably due to the fact that we do not recite the Sh'ma during that service, and we have already performed the mitzvah of wearing the טַלִית (*tallit*) during the שַׁחֲרִית (*Shaharit*) service.[23]

When one buys a new טַלִית (*tallit*), he must recite the בְּרָכָה (*b'rakhah*) of שֶׁהֶחֱיָנוּ (*Sheheheyanu*) just as he would when buying any new garment.[24] This בְּרָכָה (*b'rakhah*) should be said when inserting the צִיצָת (*tzitzit*) into the garment. If it was not recited then, it should be said when donning this טַלִית (*tallit*) for the first time.[25] It is reported that "in the days of the great (scholars)" in Renish, it was customary to call to the Torah anyone who purchased a new טַלִית (*tallit*) to demonstrate how zealously they cherished the mitzvah.[26]

There are various customs concerning when a חַזָּן (*hazzan*) wears a טַלִית (*tallit*). Among some worshipers, the חַזָּן (*hazzan*) wears a טַלִית (*tallit*) during all services.[27] Others practice that the חַזָּן (*hazzan*) wears the טַלִית (*tallit*) only when the rest of the congregation wears one. Even among the latter, he wears it during all Shabbat and holiday services. There is a practice among some for the חַזָּן (*hazzan*) not to put on the טַלִית (*tallit*) on Shabbat afternoon for the מִנְחָה (*Minhah*) service until after he recites the verse *va'ani tefilati*, etc. The reason suggested for this is that the verse speaks of this time being an acceptable moment for Hashem to answer our prayers, as the verse implies.[28]

On weekdays, when one wears a טַלִית (*tallit*) and tefillin, the former is put on first. This is so because of a principle affirmed in the Talmud that whenever there are two distinct deeds to perform, the one that is more common or done more often is performed first.[29] Since a טַלִית (*tallit*) is worn on Shabbat and holidays, when tefillin are not worn, then its use is more often and comes first. Another reason offered[30] is that the צִיצָת (*tzitzit*) are a reminder of all other commandments, as found in the Biblical precept, "and you shall look upon it and remember all the commandments of Adonai," (Num. 15:39). Interestingly enough, however, Rabbi Amram Gaon in his *Siddur* mentions putting on the tefillin and then explains the בְּרָכָה (*b'rakhah*) to be said when putting on the טַלִית (*tallit*).[31]

The Manner of Donning the Tallit

The manner of donning the טַלִית (*tallit*) and how it is worn is subject to an unlimited number of customs. The *Shulhan Arukh*[32] states that one should put on the טַלִית (*tallit*) and recite a בְּרָכָה (*b'rakhah*) while standing. The *Mishnah Berurah*[33] explains that both the בְּרָכָה (*b'rakhah*) and the donning should be performed while standing. The בְּרָכָה (*b'rakhah*) is recited standing as is every בְּרָכָה (*b'rakhah*) said on the performance of a mitzvah.[34] Standing while putting on the טַלִית (*tallit*) is derived from the similarity of the Biblical wording in the mitzvah of צִיצָת (*tzitzit*) and the mitzvah of counting the עוֹמֶר (*Omer*), where standing is required.[35] After reciting the בְּרָכָה (*b'rakhah*), one covers his head with the טַלִית (*tallit*) and tosses the צִיצָת (*tzitzit*) over his left shoulder keeping it in that position the time it takes him to walk four ells (about 6 feet or 1.8 meters).[36] It is done this way in accordance with the *Tur*,[37] who states in the name of the *Geonim* that the donning has to be in the manner of *atifat yishme'elim*, or the way the Ishmaelites wear their head garment.[38]

The *Shulhan Arukh* states that one should don his טַלִית (*tallit*) in the synagogue. The *Rema*, however, says that the prevailing custom is to don the טַלִית

(*tallit*) and tefillin at home and go to synagogue wearing them both.[39]

It is important that one examine the צִיצָת (*tzitzit*) of the טַלִית (*tallit*) before reciting the בְּרָכָה (*b'rakhah*). The usual custom is to place the טַלִית (*tallit*) over one's shoulder and check to see that the threads of the צִיצָת (*tzitzit*) are not torn or missing.[40] Before reciting the בְּרָכָה (*b'rakhah*), one should hold the טַלִית (*tallit*) in his hand ready to place it over himself. Harav Soloveitchik maintains that he should be holding it behind his back and lift it over his head so that immediately after saying the בְּרָכָה (*b'rakhah*), he can cover his head with the טַלִית (*tallit*), since it is required to recite the בְּרָכָה (*b'rakhah*) immediately preceding performance of the mitzvah.[41] The בְּרָכָה (*b'rakhah*) starts as do all בְּרָכוֹת (*b'rakhot*) before performing a mitzvah, and ends with the words, "who has commanded us to wrap ourselves with צִיצָת (*tzitzit*)." There is a difference of opinion as to whether the word should be the indefinite form *betzitzit* (with tzitzit) or the definite form *batzitzit* (with *the* tzitzit).[42] The prevailing custom is to say the latter. The Kabbalists suggest reciting two verses beginning with the words *barkhi nafshi* from the Book of Psalms (104:1-2) before reciting the בְּרָכָה (*b'rakhah*), and three verses, beginning with the words *mah yakar*, also from Psalms (38:8-11), after the בְּרָכָה (*b'rakhah*).

There are various customs concerning who should wear a טַלִית (*tallit*) during prayer. Originally only married men wore a טַלִּית (*tallit*).[43] The *Mishnah Berurah*[44] questions this practice, which is based on a statement found in *Derashot Maharil*,[45] and asks, why should a young man who is not married "sit idle and not perform this Mitzvah?" *Otzer Dinim Uminhagim*[46] quotes a source that explains that the reason unmarried men do not wear a טַלִּית (*tallit*) is so they will be readily recognizable in the synagogues and embarrassed, thus hurry and get married. According to the *Otzer*, the custom in Israel and in Egypt is for unmarried men to wear the טַלִּית (*tallit*). The procedure in Morocco is for them not to wear it. There is a custom among many communities that on the day a man gets married, his bride presents him with a טַלִּית (*tallit*).[47] There is also the practice that a man covers his head with the טַלִּית (*tallit*) during prayer only after he is married. This is based on the Biblical passage that in one instance the mitzvah of wearing צִיצָת (*tzitzit*) is followed immediately with a passage that deals with marriage.[48] *Otzer Dinim Uminhagim* further explains that there is a practice among the righteous that the learned cover their heads with the טַלִּית (*tallit*), while the non-learned merely wear it over their shoulders. The reason for this is that covering the head symbolizes that a halo of the light of the Torah, as it were, is hovering over the head of the scholar. This is similar to the custom of the *Kohanim* covering their heads with the טַלִּית (*tallit*) during the Priestly Benediction to shield them from the שְׁכִינָה (*Shekhinah*), or Divine Presence, which hovers over them during the blessings. There is a

view that one reciting mourner's קַדִּישׁ (*Kaddish*)
should wear a טַלִּית (*tallit*) out of respect.[49]

How the Tallit Should be Worn

The *Shulhan Arukh*[50] maintains that one should cover
his head with the טַלִּית (*tallit*) during prayer. The
Mishnah Berurah[51] elucidates that doing so will
humble his heart and intensify his fear of Heaven. He
states in the name of the *Bayit Hadash* that one should
keep the טַלִּית (*tallit*) over his head from the beginning
of the service until the end. However, the *Magen
Avraham*[52] says that the main mitzvah of טַלִּית (*tallit*) is
to cover the body from the shoulders down.
Accordingly, we find various practices. Some cover
their heads throughout the entire prayer, some during
certain parts of the prayers, and some not at all.[53]
Some places require anyone called to the Torah for an
עֲלִיָה (*aliyah*) to wear a טַלִּית (*tallit*).[54]

It is preferable always to keep the front צִיצת (*tzitzit*)
of the טַלִּית (*tallit*) in front and the back ones always in
the back so that he is surrounded by mitzvot.[55] In
order to be able to keep track of which are in front
and which are in back, the practice has evolved to sew
on a strip of material along the top of the טַלִּית (*tallit*)
near the part that covers the shoulders or the head.[56]
This way, one will always know which side of the
טַלִּית (*tallit*) is up and the צִיצת (*tzitzit*) will always be
on the proper side. This material is referred to as an
עֲטָרָה (*atarah*) or crown. Some people will use a fancy

designed עֲטָרָה (*atarah*) or even one made from silver or other luxurious material. Maimonides was asked a question concerning a man who embroidered the Biblical verses referring to the commandment of צִיצַת (*tzitzit*) on his טַלִית (*tallit*). The inquirer wanted to know if this is permissible. Maimonides answered that not only is it not permissible, but one may not even wear this טַלִית (*tallit*).[57]

During the Priestly Benediction, when the *Kohanim* recite the Biblical verse[58] with which they were instructed to bless the people, they extend their hands forward at shoulder level. Maimonides states[59] that the *Kohanim* should not be looking at the people, but rather be looking down, so as not to be distracted from the benediction. Similarly, the congregation should not be looking at them in order that they, too, not be distracted. Hence, the custom has evolved that the *Kohanim* pull the טַלִית (*tallit*) over their heads and over their hands.[60] In some practices, the *Kohanim* keep their hands out of the טַלִית (*tallit*) so that they should not look at their hands, and in some practices, they cover their hands to prevent the congregants from looking at their hands.

One may borrow a טַלִית (*tallit*) without obtaining permission from the owner[61] and recite the blessing over it. There is, however, an opinion that it is preferable that he keep in mind that he is only borrowing it and has no intention of making it his own even temporarily during the prayers. Under these conditions, he should not recite the blessing.[62] When someone borrows a synagogue טַלִּית (*tallit*), however, he does recite the בְּרָכָה (*b'rakhah*). A synagogue טַלִּית (*tallit*) is not considered borrowed, but belongs to everyone, and when donning one it is as if he is wearing his own, and thus a בְּרָכָה (*b'rakhah*) should be recited.

On Shabbat, after removing the טַלִּית (*tallit*), it is not proper to fold it.[63] It is suggested to fold it, however, immediately after Shabbat in order to start the week with a mitzvah.[64] Rabbi Moshe Feinstein says that, where it is permitted to carry on Shabbat, if one plans to take his טַלִּית (*tallit*) home because he does not want to leave it in the synagogue lest someone else use it and dirty it, he is then permitted to fold it. Otherwise, it will become creased and hence unseemly and unbecoming.[65]

Holiday Practices

Before *Rosh Hashanah*, the סְלִיחוֹת (*Selihot*) services (prayers of repentance) are said for at least four days. Sephardic Jews say them the entire month of אֱלוּל (*Elul*). Halakhah requires that they be said in the early morning hours before dawn. During these services, the חַזָּן (*hazzan*) wears a טַלִּית (*tallit*), since he recites the "Thirteen Attributes of the Almighty" (Ex. 34:5-7).[66] Because one does not recite a בְּרָכָה (*b'rakhah*) over the טַלִּית (*tallit*) at night, it is suggested that the חַזָּן (*hazzan*) not use his own טַלִּית (*tallit*), or that of the

synagogue, and thus not be obligated to recite the
בְּרָכָה (b'rakhah).[67] On all fast days, the "Thirteen
Attributes of the Almighty" are recited. It is thus
customary for the חַזָן (hazzan) to wear a טַלִית (tallit)
during the מִנחָה (Minhah) service, even though the
practice may normally be not to wear it during that
service.

On *Yom Kippur* night we are to wear the טַלִית (tallit)
during the מַעֲרִיב (Ma'ariv) service,[68] because we want
to be likened to the angels, who are said to appear in
white. Since one does not recite a בְּרָכָה (b'rakhah) on a
טַלִית (tallit) at night, the practice is to don it before
nightfall. In actuality, it is worn for the Kol Nidre
service and not removed until after the מַעֲרִיב
(Ma'ariv) service is completed.[69]

On *Simhat Torah*, we read the last portion of the
Torah. There are many customs associated with this
practice. It is the practice that everyone is honored
with an עֲלִיָה (aliyah), and the portion is reread to
make it possible for all congregants present to receive
an עֲלִיָה (aliyah). The last section of the portion is read
only once at the very end. It is customary to give this
last עֲלִיָה (aliyah) of the Torah to a distinguished
member of the congregation. The one so honored is
called חֲתַן תּוֹרָה (Hatan Torah), or the Groom of the
Torah. Since he is given the title of groom, a חֻפָּה
(hupah), or canopy, is erected over his head by means
of spreading a טַלִית (tallit) over everyone standing
around the Readers Table. The next Torah portion

read immediately following the conclusion of the Torah is the beginning of the Torah. Another distinguished person is honored with this Torah reading. He is given the title *Hatan Bereshit* ~ or the Groom of בְּרֵאשִׁית (*Bereshit*) ~ בְּרֵאשִׁית (*Bereshit*) being the first Hebrew word in the Torah. He is also covered with a חֻפָּה (*hupah*) by means of a טַלִּית (*tallit*), as was the previous reader. It is also customary to call up all the children under the age of bar mitzvah for an עֲלִיָה (*aliyah*) together with one of the elders of the congregation. This עֲלִיָה (*aliyah*) is the one before חֲתַן תּוֹרָה (*Hatan Torah*) and is known as *Kol Hane'arim*. In order to unite all the children with the gentleman honored with this aliyah, a טַלִּית (*tallit*) is spread over all their heads.[70]

On תִּשְׁעָה בְּאָב (*Tishah b'Av*) ~ the fast of the 9th of *Av* ~ the day that commemorates the destruction of the First and Second Temple in Jerusalem, Jews are required to fast. Since this is such a tragic remembrance, the custom dictates that we do not wear a טַלִּית (*tallit*) or tefillin during the morning service. Instead, we wear them for the מִנְחָה (*Minhah*) service.[71]

The סַנְדָק (*Sandek*)[72] at a בְּרִית מִילָה (*Brit Milah*), or circumcision, wears a טַלִּית (*tallit*).[73] If the בְּרִית (*brit*) takes place on תִּשְׁעָה בְּאָב (*Tishah b'Av*) in the morning, the סַנְדָק (*Sandek*) does not wear the טַלִּית (*tallit*).[74]

Marriage Customs

Our practice at a wedding is that the ceremony takes place under a canopy. The canopy is formed by a piece of material stretched over four posts. This canopy is known as the חֻפָּה (*hupah*). In some places, a טַלִּית (*tallit*) is spread over the four posts. There was a custom among some Jews that the groom wears a טַלִּית (*tallit*) during the ceremony and puts it over the head of his bride. This, they believed, was the true meaning of חֻפָּה (*hupah*), and this act indicates that the groom is taking the bride as his wife under his protection.[75]

Burial

It is the practice in most communities to bury a departed male in a טַלִּית (*tallit*).[76] This is a custom symbolically indicating that the individual fulfilled the mitzvah of טַלִּית (*tallit*) during his lifetime.[77] Generally in Israel this is not the practice.... In Israel, the departed is covered with a טַלִּית (*tallit*) when being carried to the cemetery, but it is removed before he is placed in the grave.[78] In the Diaspora, where usually the deceased is buried with a טַלִּית (*tallit*), it is rendered unfit by removing one of the צִיצִת (*tzitzit*),[79] since the departed is not obligated to wear a טַלִּית (*tallit*). In the Talmud,[80] a story is related that Rabbi Hiyya and Rabbi Jonathan were once walking about in a cemetery, and the blue fringes צִיצִת (*tzitzit*) of Rabbi Jonathan were trailing on the ground. Said Rabbi Hiyya to him, "Lift it up, so that they (the dead) should not say, 'Tomorrow they are coming to join us and now they are insulting us.'" The meaning is that they were demonstrating that they are performing a mitzvah while the dead are exempt from it. Based on this incident, the *Shulhan Arukh*[81] states that one should not go into a cemetery when his צִיצָת (*tzitzit*) are exposed.

The Tallit in Rabbinic Homiletics

The טַלִּית (*tallit*) occupies a dominant role in the homiletic discussions in the Talmud and the midrashim. Our Rabbis tell us, for example, that when Korah rebelled against Moshe's leadership in the journeys through the wilderness, he wanted to ridicule Moshe. They find a definite correlation between the passage that deals with the mitzvah of צִיצָת (*tzitzit*) and the fact that the story of the rebellion of Korah follows immediately in the Torah. The Rabbis say that Korah confronted Moshe and asked him concerning the halakhic requirement to attach צִיצָת (*tzitzit*) and have a blue thread, or תְּכֵלֶת (*tekhelet*), on a four-cornered garment. "If a cloak is entirely of blue, is the garment obligated in the mitzvah of צִיצָת (*tzitzit*)?" he asked. Moshe answered that it is subject to the obligation of צִיצָת (*tzitzit*). Mockingly, Korah said, "A garment that is entirely composed of blue cannot free itself of the obligation of צִיצָת (*tzitzit*), yet four blue threads do free it."[82]

According to our midrashic Sages, the reason Jews merited the privilege of the mitzvah of צִיצָת (*tzitzit*) relates back to the story of Noah. After the flood, when Noah and his family left the Ark, Noah planted a vineyard and drank of the wine and became drunk. His son Ham saw his father's nakedness and told his brothers. Shem, together with his brother Japhet, took a garment and walked backwards and covered their father's nakedness (Gen. 9:20-23). Since it was Shem who initiated the action of taking the garment to cover his father, his descendants were rewarded with the mitzvah of צִיצָת (*tzitzit*).[83]

The Talmud and the Midrash in a number of places visualize the Almighty as wrapped in a טַלִּית (*tallit*). Rabbi Yohanan said, "Were it not written in the Scriptures, 'And Adonai passed by before him and proclaimed…' (Ex. 34:6)[84] it would be impossible for us to say such a thing. This verse teaches us that the Holy One, blessed be He, wrapped Himself like the messenger of the congregation (hazzan) and showed Moses the order of prayer."[85] The *Midrash Rabbah*, likewise, tells us that Rabbi Simeon the son of Yehozadok asked Rabbi Samuel the son of Rabbi Nahman, "Since I heard that you are an expert *haggadist*, tell me, whence comes light unto the world?" He answered him, "The Holy One, blessed be He, wrapped Himself as in a garment (tallit), and the whole world shone with the splendor of His majesty."[86] We are also told that when the Children of Israel were leaving the Land of Egypt, they were

instructed about the new calendar they were to follow
(Ex. 12:2). In reference to this passage, the midrash tells
us that Rabbi Hiyya said in the name of Rabbi
Yohanan, "The Holy One, blessed be He, wrapped
Himself in a טַלִית (*tallit*) with צִיצַת (*tzitzit*), and placed
Moses at one side and Aaron on the other, and called
upon Michael and Gabriel and made them witnesses
of the moon, as it were, and asked them, 'How did
you see the moon?'"[87] What this means is that the
Almighty called together a *Bet Din* to establish the
new moon and thus to instruct Moses about the
procedure for this responsibility.

As mentioned above, when the Holy One revealed
His glory to Moses, He was enveloped in a טַלִית
(*tallit*), as it were. Our Sages tell us, based on the
passage in the Torah that commands us, "and you
shall walk in God's ways," that it is our obligation to
try to emulate the traits of the Almighty. Since Moses
was shown the manner in which the Holy One was
garbed, we, too, must imitate God and wear the טַלִית
(*tallit*) as a sign of our respect for the Almighty. The
טַלִית (*tallit*) with the צִיצַת (*tzitzit*) attached to its four
corners serves as a constant reminder of our
obligation to fulfill all the commandments given us
by the Holy One. This is the explanation the Torah
gives for this mitzvah as we recite daily in the Sh'ma,
"and you will look upon it, and remember all the
commandments of Adonai, and do them" (Num. 15:39).
The טַלִית (*tallit*) has become the symbol of the Jewish

people and served as the blueprint of the Israeli flag in modern days.

---

[1] Rashi *ad loc* claims it is called *tzitzit* because of the threads that hang down from it. He compares it to a passage in Ezekiel (8:3), which reads: "and I was taken by a lock (*tzitzit*) of my head." He offers a second derivation of the word based on the command to "look at it." Here the root of the word, he says, would be similar to the passage in the Song of Songs (2:9) that reads: "peering (*metzitz*) through the lattice." Onkelos translates *kruspidin*, which Jastrow translates as "edge," "border," "fringe." Even-Shoshan, in his Hebrew dictionary, explains it to mean "a bunch of threads." William Gesenius, in his Lexicon, understands it to come from the word *tzitz*, which he translates as "flowerlike" or "winglike."

[2] These threads had to be colored from dyestuffs extracted from the *hilazon* (a worm). According to the Rabbis of the Talmud (Meg. 6a), one of the primary occupations of the tribe of Zebulon was the extraction of the dye from the hilazon that was found on the shores of their territories.

[3] *Mitzvah* 386.

[4] The question of a garment with more than four corners is discussed in the Talmud (Zeb. 18b). Two Tannaitic positions are rendered. One position is that four corners or more require tzitzit, and another opinion states that only a garment with four corners requires tzitzit. If the garment has three or five or more, it is exempt.

[5] See Shab. 25b, where the Talmud describes the practice of Rabbi Judah ben Il'ai as follows: on the eve of the Sabbath, a basin filled with hot water was brought to him, and he washed his face, hands, and feet, and he wrapped himself and sat in fringed linen robe, and was like an angel of the Lord of Hosts.

---

[6] *Shabbat* 10a.

[7] *Ibid.* The term used in this passage is *gelima*, which actually means "cloak" and is another term for *tallit*. We also learn there that some Rabbis reacted in the opposite manner, removing the garment so that it should be visible at all times.

[8] Orah Hayyim 22,1.

[9] This is a small four-cornered garment worn specifically for the sole purpose of fulfilling the mitzvah of tzitzit. Some people wear this under their outer shirt, and some wear it over their outer garment so that it should be visible at all times.

[10] *Zohar*, Shelah. See *Sefer Hazohar*, Vilna 5655, p. 175.

[11] In the third paragraph.

[12] The *Arukh Hashulhan* (Orah Hayyim 8:1) says that this opinion is based on the statement in the Talmud (Ber. 14b), "If one recites the Sh'ma without tefillin, it is as if he bore false witness against himself." The same reasoning is applied to tzitzit. He claims, however, that the Talmud is referring specifically to tefillin, which one is obligated to wear, but not to tzitzit, for which there is no mitzvah or obligation unless one is wearing a four-cornered garment.

[13] Shmuel Pinchas Gelbard, *Rite and Reason*, English Translation, Petach Tikvah, 1998, p.22.

[14] Men. 39b.

[15] *Aseh doheh lo ta'aseh.*

[16] Yeb. 4a.

[17] *Shulhan Arukh*, O.H. 8,14. In *Ta'ame Haminhagim* (Rabbi Avraham Yitzhak Sperling, Eshkol, Jerusalem, 1957, p. 314, footnote) the suggestion is made that upon reciting the b'rakhah when first donning the tallit, one should intentionally think that it is only for this one time, and if he should remove the tallit, he will again recite a b'rakhah. This way he avoids the two contradictory opinions.

[18] Num. 15:39.

[19] Men. 43b.

[20] The exception to this rule is *Kol Nidre* night on Yom Kippur.

[21] Ber. 20b, " ...women are exempt from all positive mitzvot that are dependent on a definite time."

[22] See Men. 43a.

[23] There are times when the tallit is worn during Minhah, such as on Tishah b'Av. This will be discussed later.

[24] *Shulhan Arukh*, Orah Hayyim 22,1.

[25] *Ibid.*, Rema.

[26] See *Ta'ame Haminhagim*, p. 157, footnote.

[27] According to the *Magen Avraham*, Orah Hayyim, 18,2, this is based on the midrash that says when the Almighty showed Moshe Rabeinu the manner of prayer, He wrapped Himself in a tallit. See more about this midrash below.

[28] *Lekute Maharih*, Israel Haim Friedman, 1923, p. 145.

[29] Ber. 51b.

---

[30] Eisenstein, *A Digest of Jewish Laws and Customs*, New York, 1917, p. 152.

[31] *Seder Rav Amram Gaon*, edited by Daniel Goldschmit, Mosad Haraav Kook, Jerusalem, 1971, p. 5. From the *Zohar* (Vilna edition, 1882, Bemidbar, p. 220b), it also appears that the tefillin precede the tallit. However, it may be explained that both Rav Amram Gaon and the *Zohar* mention the tefillin before the tallit as referring to them in the order of their importance, and not necessarily the order of putting them on.

[32] Orah Hayyim, 8,1.

[33] *Ibid.* s.v. 2.

[34] See Menachem Raab, "When Standing is Appropriate in Prayer," *Journal of Jewish Music and Liturgy*, XIX, 1996-1997.

[35] See *Mishnah Berurah* 8,1. The *Mishnah Berurah* states, however, that if one did not stand during the b'rakhah or while putting on the tallit, he nevertheless did fulfill his obligation, *ibid.* s.v. 2.

[36] *Ibid.* s.v. 4.

[37] O.H. 8.

[38] The *Chabad* custom is to cover the eyes as well. See *Sefer Haminhagim, Minhage Chabad*, Brooklyn, 1967, p. 3.

[39] O.H. 25,2.

[40] *Shulhan Arukh*, O.H. 8,9. According to *Sefer Haminhagim, Minhage Chabad*, op. cit., p. 3, one should place the tallit on his right shoulder.

[41] *Nefesh Harav*, Hershel Schachter, Reshit Yerushalayim, Jerusalem, 1994, p. 104.

[42] See *Birkhe Yosef*, Chaim Yosef Azulai, O.H. 8,4.

[43] *Otzer Yisrael*, s.v. *tallit*.

[44] 17,10. The *Be'ur Hetev* 17,4 suggests that before marriage one should wear the tallit but not cover his head with it. He brings various sources for this opinion, but rejects it.

[45] *Hilkhot Nesu'in*. His reason for this practice is based on the fact that the Torah, in declaring the mitzvah of tzitzit, states, "you shall make twisted threads upon the four corners of your garment" (Deut. 22:12), and immediately follows with the portion dealing with "If a man takes a wife...."

[46] Eisenstein, *A Digest of Jewish Laws and Customs*, p. 151.

[47] *Ta'ame Haminhagim*, p. 405.

[48] Deut. 22:12-13. See *Ta'ame Haminhagim*, p. 410.

[49] *Elya Rabbah*, O.H. 18,2.

[50] *Orah Hayyim* 8,2.

[51] *Ibid*, 8,4.

[52] *Ibid*, 8,2.

[53] Rabbi Soloveitchik reported in the name of his grandfather Rabbi Haim that he would cover his head before *Kaddish* and *Barekhu*, and then remove it from his head for the recitation of the *Sh'ma*, and then cover his head again for the *Amidah*. The reason he did not want to cover his head during the *Sh'ma* was

---

based on the *Midrash* brought by the *Turei Zahav* (*Orah Hayyim* 8,3), which relates that the Almighty said to Israel, Behold I did not require you to recite the *Sh'ma* uncovering your head (but as "you sit in your house and when you walk by the way"). The meaning is that the *Sh'ma* should be recited in your normal way of attire. Normally, one does not wear the tallit over his head. See *Nefesh Harav*, op. cit. p. 104.

[54] *Ta'ame Haminhagim*, p. 155, footnote.

[55] *Shulhan Arukh, Orah Hayyim* 8,4.

[56] *Mishnah Berurah* 8,9.

[57] *She'elot Utshuvot Harambam*, No. 168.

[58] Num. 6:24-26.

[59] Laws of *Tefillah* 14,7.

[60] *Rema*, O.H. 128,23. The *Mishnah Berurah, ad loc,* explains that in the time of the Temple, the reason for not looking at the hands of the *Kohanim* was because the *Kohanim* invoked the Ineffable Name of the Almighty, and the *Shekhinah*, or Divine Presence, hovered over their hands. Today, the reason for not looking at them is not to be distracted.

[61] *Shulhan Arukh, Orah Hayyim* 14,4. The *Mishnah Berurah* s.v. 13 explains that a person is satisfied that someone can fulfill a mitzvah with his possessions.

[62] *Magen Avraham, Orah Hayyim* 14,8. This is based on the Talmudic statement (Hulin 110b) that says "a borrowed tallit is exempt from having tzitzit for thirty days." Tosafot (*ad loc*, s.v. *tallit*) says that, likewise, one does not recite a b'rakhah on a borrowed tallit.

---

[63] Talmud Shab. 113a and *Magen Avraham*, O.H. 302,6.

[64] *Ta'ame Haminhagim*, para. 424.

[65] *Igrot Moshe*, O.H. Vol. 5, No. 20 *Mah.*

[66] *Magen Avraham*, O.H. 18,2 states in the name of the *Levush* that whenever the Thirteen Attributes are recited, the hazzan should wear the tallit, although the *Magen Avraham* himself maintains that he should wear it at all services.

[67] *Magen Avraham*, O.H. 581,3 and *Mishnah Berurah* s.v. 6.

[68] *Rema*, O.H. 18,1 and *Mishnah Berurah* 519,4.

[69] *Mishnah Berurah* 18,6.

[70] Rabbi Eliezer Judah Waldenburg, in his Responsa *Tzitz Eliezer*, Vol. 16, No. 8, questions the validity of using a tallit to make a canopy, since this is like building a tent, which is prohibited on a holiday. He relates that in Italy, where he was born, they used an actual wedding canopy for this purpose.

[71] *Shulhan Arukh* O.H. 555,1.

[72] The person who holds the baby during the circumcision.

[73] *Sefer Otzer Habrit*, Yosef David Visberg, Jerusalem, 5646, Vol. 1, p. 138. The reason for this custom given by Shmuel Pinchas Gelbard in *Rite and Reason*, op. cit. p. 585, is "to honor and exult the mitzvah of *Milah*." It is also customary for the father of the baby and the *mohel* who performs the circumcision to wear a tallit, though there is no source for this custom.

---

[74] *Sha'arey Teshuva*, O.H. 265,12. He does mention, however, that he had seen a Sandek who did wear a tallit at a brit on Tishah b'Av, and he did not stop him.

[75] *Sefer Hanesu'in Kehilkhatam*, Binyamin Adler, Jerusalem, Second Edition, 5745, p. 245; also pp. 347, 376, and 588.

[76] See *Mahzor Vitri*, Chap. 278.

[77] *Igrot Moshe, Yoreh De'ah* Vol. 1, No. 244, *Akh*, etc.

[78] *Gesher Hahayyim*, Rabbi Yekhiel Mikhael Tuketzinsky, Jerusalem, 5720, p. 105.

[79] The *Mahzor Vitri* mentions that a certain Rabbi Eliyahu instructed his children not to remove the tzitzit.

[80] Ber. 18a.

[81] *Orah Hayyim* 23,1.

[82] *Midrash Rabbah*, Numbers 18,3 and T. Yerushalmi, San. 10,1 (27d).

[83] *Bereshit Rabbah*, 36,6.

[84] The passage relates how Moses prayed for the Almighty to reveal to him a greater degree of understanding of the Almighty. He is directed where to stand, and Hashem passes before him and instructs him how to pray and teaches him the "Thirteen Attributes of the Almighty."

[85] R.H. 17b. Rabbi Yom Tov Ben Abraham Ishbili (known as the *Ritva*) explains this passage as a vision that Moses saw through his prophesies. Rabbi Shmuel Eliezer Halevi Idilish (known as the *Maharsha*) also explains this passage in the same manner, and

further points out that, according to the Kabbalists, the tallit that the Holy One wore was the same one He wore when He created light, as quoted *infra*. For other explanations, see Talmud Babli, Adin Steinsaltz R.H. 17b footnote.

[86] *Ber. Rabbah* 3,4; *Lev. Rabbah* 31,7. This same midrash appears in other places with certain variations. See *Tanhuma, VaYakhel* 6; *Yalkut Shimoni, Tehillim* 862, and others.

[87] *Yalkut Shimoni* 191.

On Wearing Tallit and Tefillin
Dvora E. Weisberg

When I was seventeen, I asked my grandfather where
I could buy tefillin. He told me that "girls don't wear
tefillin." When I persisted, saying that I already was
wearing tefillin, he told me that I wouldn't be able to
afford them. After I said I was prepared to spend my
entire summer salary, my grandfather, convinced I
was serious, bought me the tefillin. The next morning
he was in מִנְיָן (*minyan*), bragging to the other men
about his granddaughter, who was "so religious, she
even puts on tefillin."

My decision to wear tallit and tefillin was not
particularly well thought out. The camp where I
worked listed them as optional equipment for
women, and I was intrigued. Given my personality, I
probably became more intrigued as various relatives
protested. If I knew little about the halakhic issues
surrounding women's observance of time-bound

positive mitzvot in general, and of tallit and tefillin in particular, I learned quickly. I was constantly called upon to defend my decision halakhically. I also had to deal with people's claims that I was offending them by my actions, even if those actions were halakhically permissible. During my first month in college, a man offered to buy my tefillin to stop me from wearing them. I found most frustrating the fact that many people ascribed motives to my wearing tallit and tefillin without asking me what my intentions actually were.

When I daven in tallit and tefillin, I am not trying to make a feminist gesture or prove that I can "pray like a man." I began to observe these mitzvot out of a desire to serve God by fulfilling God's commandments. It never occurred to me that the need to be reminded of God's presence in regular, concrete ways was limited to men. I felt, and still feel, that every mitzvah I perform strengthens the bond between me and my Creator. The recitation of "And I shall betroth you to me forever..." as I bind tefillin on my arm, the awareness of being enveloped in a tallit, evoke very powerful feelings in me. I can no more consider discarding my tefillin than I could consider eating pork; I regard all the mitzvot I observe as obligatory.

I realize that wearing tallit and tefillin is a highly visible action and one that arouses strong emotions in other people. I know that what I intend to be my personal commitment becomes a public statement every time I enter a synagogue. While part of me responds to the opportunity to represent a change in women's patters of observance, there is also a part that sometimes longs to be an unremarkable member of the congregation.

My grandfather died two years ago. I have put his tefillin away, to be given someday to my first child, his great grandchild. I like to think my grandfather would be no less pleased if the child is a daughter rather than a son. I want to believe that his acceptance of my observance was not only a grandfather's pride in his granddaughter but also a reflection of his ability to accept the idea that women can be as committed to mitzvot they have accepted out of religious conviction as they are to those they have observed for centuries. This is all I would ask or expect from him...or from anyone else.

From Tzitzit to Tallit
Moshe Tutnauer

Introduction

The inspiration to study and teach about the tallit came from a young girl named Alina Weinstein who lives in Chernovitz, in the Ukraine. Alina was among some fifty people present at a meeting held in May 1991. The goal of that meeting was to inspire grandparents, parents, children, and teachers to renew Jewish learning in Chernovitz by starting a TALI (Conservative) Jewish Day School.

At that gathering, I used my tallit as a symbol of Jewish life. Some of the older people present had distant memories of a parent who used a tallit. Most of the people under fifty had never seen one. Nobody owned one. I told those gathered how, twenty years earlier, in 1971, my wife, Margie, and our sons Nahum and Roney had to "smuggle" several tallitot into Moscow. Now Jews are free to use a tallit. So I demonstrated how traditional Jews begin the day by closing their eyes and wrapping themselves in a tallit. This profound moment spent alone with God is an integral part of the Jewish tradition. Then I draped my tallit on my shoulders, opened my eyes, and looked into the faces of everyone present. A Jew needs a moment with God, but leads a life among people. Communal responsibility is an integral part of the Jewish tradition.

The meeting was successful, the school was opened and in the summer of 1991 a Ramah camp was opened near Moscow. The following summer, young people from the Chernovitz school traveled to Moscow (32 hours on the train) to be part of Ramah's second year. Alina was one of them.

By that time she had learned to speak Hebrew and to chant the morning services. During the summer, she was taught how to make a tallit. She made one for me, telling me to show that tallit wherever I went. No longer did American Jews have to sneak tallitot into the Former Soviet Union. Now young people there were making their own tallitot and exporting them to the rest of the Jewish world.

שֶׁהֶחֱיָנוּ וְקִיְּמָנוּ וְהִגִּיעָנוּ לַזְּמַן הַזֶּה

Shehecheyanu vekeyimanu vehigianu lazman hazeh
Thanks to God for keeping us alive,
sustaining us, and bringing us to this moment.

Just as the kind of clothes we wear reveals much about our character, the kind of tallit we wear, when and if we wear it, makes a statement about our Jewish identity. You may have given some thought to the kind of tallit you want, but have you thought about what it all means? Why have Jews worn this strange garment for centuries? When do we wear it? What meaning has it had throughout our history, and what can it mean for us today? What is the origin of the tradition, and what actually makes a tallit a tallit?

Today the tallit is seen as an important Jewish symbol, but it was not always so popular in North America. When the Reform movement took root in this country in the late 1800s, Reform Jews seemed uncomfortable wearing the traditional Jewish articles, and most Reform synagogues did away with the kippah, tefillin, and tallit. Conservative Jewish men from the age of bar mitzvah continued to wear a tallit when they attended services, but it was usually the small, rayon version provided by the synagogue. Orthodox Jewish men always wore a tallit when they prayed, but only after they were married.

Now the tallit is experiencing a rebirth. Many Reform synagogues provide tallitot for their members. Almost all Reform rabbis wear a tallit, as do those congregants who go up to the Torah for an עֲלִיָּה (*aliyah*). Today many more Conservative Jews own a tallit. A growing number of women in the Reform and Conservative movements are now choosing to wear a tallit. Some young people and adults are making their own tallitot, or buying personalized ones. At your synagogue, you can see tallitot in different sizes, styles, and colors, on women and men, young and old. On Simhat Torah, you may see all the children in the synagogue called up to be blessed under a tallit.

So when you wrap yourself in the tallit, you are carrying on an ageless tradition and joining countless Jews all over the world who are performing this mitzvah.

The Tallit as Clothing

The tallit is basically an article of clothing. What makes it special is that it is four-cornered and has צִיצָת (*tzitzit*) attached to each corner. We will understand the tallit better if first we look at the role that clothing has played since the days of the Bible.

Why Clothing

According to the Torah, the first humans walked the earth without clothing, like the animals. The Garden of Eden's temperature was always moderate, so who needed clothing? People began wearing clothing after Eve and Adam sinned by eating from the Tree of Knowledge. Perhaps their new knowledge was their recognition that men and women were different, and they wanted to hide those differences.

Another explanation is that after sinning against God, they put on clothing to hide themselves from God and from each other. Interestingly, the Hebrew letters which make up the word for clothing ~ בֶּגֶד (*beged*) ~ are the same letters that make up the word traitor ~ בּוֹגֵד (*boged*). Maybe one of the reasons that people wear clothing is to hide themselves, their thoughts, and their weaknesses.

Clothing as a Symbol

The Bible talks about clothing as a symbol of a person's identity. It tells us that men should not wear female clothing and women should not wear male clothing. Priests have several sets of special clothing that they wear on special occasions. Kings also have a special wardrobe that denotes their status. In the Book of Genesis, when Joseph is appointed to a high-ranking position in Egypt, Pharaoh gives him special clothing. In the Scroll of Esther, when Haman thinks the king is about to honor him, he asks to be outfitted in special clothing. It seems that Haman thought that clothing makes the man. So our clothing does more than protect us from the elements of nature; it tells the world who we are and who we want to be.

Clothing is also a sign of belonging. People wear all sorts of uniforms that send all sorts of messages. Think of what you can tell about a girl at school wearing a letter jacket, or torn jeans, or black army boots. And what about a guy who always wears Save-the-Endangered Species t-shirts, or a celebrity who wears a red ribbon on his lapel? What are they telling us about their values? Sometimes people are forced to wear special clothing, like the yellow stars that the Jews of Germany were forced to wear during World War II. The Nazis intended the Star of David to be a label of humiliation; many Jews wore it as a symbol of pride.

Color and Fabric

The color and fabric of our clothing is often as important as the clothing itself. Clothing made from expensive material, like silk or linen, is worn by important people or on special occasions. Purple or royal blue often symbolizes majesty and political stature. During the days that the Temple stood in Jerusalem, the High Priest used to wear all white on Yom Kippur as a sign of purity. If you were at High Holiday services, you may remember that the Torah covers were white and most of the congregants wore white kippot, symbolizing their desire to become spiritually pure people and start the new year with a clean slate.

The color of clothing can also indicate how you feel on a certain occasion. A "black tie affair" means that this is a very special occasion. But black at a funeral has a different meaning.

If our clothing makes such clear statements about us, what are we saying when we put on a tallit? Just what does a rectangular garment with some odd fringes on the corners express?

The Tallit as Mitzvah

One of the things you do when you put on a tallit is fulfilling a mitzvah. The actual mitzvah is to make צִיצִת (*tzitzit*) for the corners of our clothing. We will talk more about the צִיצִת (*tzitzit*) itself in the next section, but first let us try to understand the role of mitzvah in Judaism.

Within Judaism there is a basic assumption that human nature is good. As Jews, we believe that each of us can strive for and achieve holiness if we behave in a fair and righteous way. God gave us the Torah to help us do this. The mitzvot contained in the Torah are our guides on the path to holiness.

According to tradition, there are 613 mitzvot; 248 of them are positive acts that we are commanded to do, and 365 are negative acts that we are commanded not to do. The rabbis find hidden meanings in numbers. They claim that there are 248 organs and limbs in the human body, so symbolically, there is a mitzvah to be done by each part of our body. There are 365 days in the year, suggesting symbolically that each day brings a temptation to do wrong, which we must try to resist.

Mitzvot are a sign of God's love for the Jewish people. They were given to us because God believes we are capable of living lives filled with holiness, justice, and righteousness. For us, mitzvot are a sign of our spiritual connection with God. When we fulfill a mitzvah and obey the word of God, it is our way of trying to be close to God. The Jewish attitude towards mitzvot is summed up in the blessing recited before doing a mitzvah: we praise God for making our lives a little more spiritual, a little more holy, by giving us specific deeds to perform. Performing mitzvot also helps us to remember our tradition and who we are. Once when I was in Moscow, I had dinner with a group of Jews who had almost forgotten their tradition. Because they were so afraid of anti-Semitism, they had tried to "shield" their children from anything Jewish, so the younger generation of their families knew nothing about Jewish customs. At one point in the conversation I asked the people around the table if any of them had any Jewish memories. One woman, in her mid seventies, closed her eyes. A smile came to her face as she made circles with her hands just as her grandmother had done when lighting Shabbat candles so many years ago. Another woman, around the same age, closed her eyes and made winding motions around her arm. She was imitating what she had seen her grandfather do when he put on tallit and tefillin. The only memories that had survived were of their grandparents performing mitzvot.

Now let's summarize. We have seen that clothing sends a message. How much of our body do we want to expose and why? Why, also, do we choose a certain fabric, color, or shape? Why, indeed, do we choose to wear certain clothing at certain occasions? Because our friends are doing the same, or because some magazine told us that this is the "in" thing to do, or because we are Jews and want to feel part of our people's history, or because it is a mitzvah and we are fulfilling God's commandment?

The Mitzvah of Tzitzit:
What We Know from the Bible

Now, let's take a look at the mitzvah of צִיצָת (*tzitzit*). The commandment to make צִיצָת (*tzitzit*) is found in Numbers, Chapter 15:37-41:

> *Adonai spoke to Moses, saying: Speak to the Israelite people and instruct them to make for themselves fringes on the corners of their garments throughout the ages; let them attach a cord of blue to the fringe at each corner. That shall be your fringe; look at it and recall all the commandments of the Lord and observe them, so that you do not follow your heart and eyes in your lustful urge. Thus you shall be reminded to observe all My commandments and to be holy to your God. I Adonai am your God, who brought you out of the land of Egypt to be your God: I, Adonai your God.*

Another version of this commandment is found in Deuteronomy, Chapter 22:12:

> *You shall make tassels on the four corners of the*
> *garment with which you cover yourself.*

Let's look more closely at the text of the mitzvah, phrase by phrase.

> *Adonai spoke to Moses, saying: Speak to the Israelite*
> *people and instruct them to make for themselves*
> *fringes on the corners of their garments throughout*
> *the ages; let them attach a cord of blue to the fringe*
> *at each corner.*

"make for themselves fringes (tzitzit)" ~

The Biblical commandment is very personal. Although addressed to the entire People of Israel, it commands that each person make צִיצָת (*tzitzit*) for himself/herself. Parents love the gifts that their children make for them. The emotional value of something homemade ~ both for the person making it and the person receiving it ~ is much greater than that of a store-bought gift. Making צִיצָת (*tzitzit*) with our own hands increases their emotional value for us, and gives us an opportunity to physically create our own personal connection to God.

The Word *Tzitzit*

The Torah's mitzvah does not mention the word tallit. It says instead to make fringes (צִיצָת - *tzitzit)* at the corners of our garments. Well, what does that strange sounding word צִיצָת (*tzitzit*) really mean? Surprise! No one knows for sure.

Some scholars suggest that צִיצָת (*tzitzit*) comes from a word meaning "to look upon" and that the צִיצָת (*tzitzit*) are objects meant to attract our attention.

Others suggest there may be a connection between צִיצָת (*tzitzit*) and the *tzitz* that was part of the High Priest's headdress. A blue cord (פְּתִיל תְּכֵלֶת - *petil tekhelet*) connected the tzitz to the headpiece worn by the Priest. Its purpose was "that Aaron may take away any sin" to "win acceptance ... before the Lord." Perhaps both the tzitz and the צִיצָת (*tzitzit*) may have been designed to protect the wearer against evil influences. Archaeologists point to a similar word in the ancient language of Akkadian. That word referred to individually designed objects that people attached to their garment to serve as a personal seal or sign of recognition.

Finally, there are scholars who believe that the word means something that grows from the head, like hair. Perhaps there are many explanations for the word because no one of them is thoroughly convincing. In some ways, the tradition incorporates all four suggested meanings; the first two explanations are evident in the way a tallit looks.

Hair-Like
When you look closely at a tallit, you will see clumps of material hanging like hairs from the tallit's narrow edges. These are the צִיצָת (*tzitzit*).

Attract Attention
But your attention will be really attracted to the corner of the tallit, because something special is hanging from each corner. A closer inspection reveals that a hole has been made in the material and that four stings have been inserted through that hole. One of these strings, longer than the others, was round around the other three to form a series of rows and knots. This is the corner tzitzit ~ *tzitzit hakanaf.*

"on the corners of their garments" ~
In the ancient world, long before sewing machines were invented, people's wardrobes often consisted of large pieces of rectangular material that were draped, tied, or belted in different ways. Jews were commanded to place fringes (צִיצָת - *tzitzit*) on the corners of these garments. The modern clothing we ordinarily wear is exempt from the mitzvah of צִיצָת (*tzitzit*) because it does not usually have four corners. That's why the tallit developed its present form. It is a special garment, similar to ancient garments that had four corners. When we pray, we wear the tallit. We have on a garment which requires צִיצָת (*tzitzit*).

Many Jews also wear a small, four-cornered garment with צִיצָת (*tzitzit*) under their regular clothing. In that way they can fulfill the commandment of צִיצָת (*tzitzit*) all day regardless of their outer clothing's shape. The garment is called אַרְבַּע כַּנְפוֹת (*arba kanfot*) ~ four corners ~ or טַלִית קָטָן (*tallit katan*) ~ small tallit. Sometimes the person lets the צִיצָת (*tzitzit*) hang outside of his outer shirt so that he can *"look at it and recall all the commandments of Adonai."*

"throughout the ages"~
Tradition has given the צִיצָת (*tzitzit*) and the tallit a special role in life cycle events. A father wears a tallit at his son's בְּרִית (*brit*). Parents may also wear tallitot at their daughter's שִׂמְחַת בַּת (*simchat bat*). In many North American communities, children receive their first tallit as a gift from their parents or from their congregation at the time of becoming bar or bat mitzvah. It is also a custom for a bride to give her groom a tallit before the marriage so that it can be used during the marriage ceremony. Many Jews are buried in a tallit. Just as Jews of all ages are united by the tallit, Jews of all generations are connected by it. The צִיצָת (*tzitzit*) has been present throughout all the periods of Jewish history, and it will continue to be an important symbol in generations to come. The fact that צִיצָת (*tzitzit*) are once again being made in the former Soviet Union proves their importance in connecting the past with the future.

"attach a cord of blue"~
The Hebrew word for the particular shade of blue used in connection with צִיצָת (*tzitzit*) is תְּכֵלֶת (*tekhelet*).

It is often mentioned in the Bible along with another color, *argaman*. Both are shades of purple, but argaman is closer to red and תְּכֵלֶת (*tekhelet*) is closer to blue. Both of these colors symbolize majesty and nobility, and are often found in places of political or spiritual importance. The presence of תְּכֵלֶת (*tekhelet*) in the צִיצָת (*tzitzit*) demonstrates its importance.

Scholars believe that in the ancient world תְּכֵלֶת (*tekhelet*) was made from a dye excreted by the glands of a snail. Making the dye required a large number of snails and many hours of skilled labor. A document from the 5th century BCE indicates that תְּכֵלֶת (*tekhelet*) cost forty times more than ordinary dyes.

Hundreds of years later, in the time of the Mishnah (200 CE), the indigo plant from India was introduced into Eretz Yisrael. It provided a much less expensive, though lower quality, תְּכֵלֶת (*tekhelet*). A set of צִיצָת (*tzitzit*) made with the less expensive indigo תְּכֵלֶת (*tekhelet*), dating back to the 1st century, was actually discovered by archaeologists in Israel in the Caves of Bar Kochba. When you visit Israel, you will be able to see them on display at the Israel Museum. You will see that the blue dye has definitely faded!

Gradually, because of the expense and tedious process, ordinary people could no longer afford to use תְּכֵלֶת (*tekhelet*). The garment which was supposed to show that ordinary people were entitled to wear the colors of Kings and Priests, soon became too expensive for ordinary people. That's why the rabbis permitted them to make all-white צִיצָת (*tzitzit*).

Once תְּכֵלֶת (*tekhelet*) was no longer used, the complicated process of making it was forgotten. Centuries later, in the 1800s, a renewed interest in the Biblical תְּכֵלֶת (*tekhelet*) emerged. Chemists, rabbis, archaeologists, and others began searching for the lost snail that was the source of תְּכֵלֶת (*tekhelet*). Several people came close to figuring out the secret, but there were always tiny details that were not quite right. Finally, about twenty years ago, a professor at Tel Aviv University put all of the historical, geographic, biological, and chemical clues together and definitively declared that the *Murex Trunculus* species of the snail was the one that everyone had been seeking. Over the last two decades, many people have been working hard at re-establishing the special dyeing process. There is even a non-profit *P'til Tekhelet* Foundation that provides תְּכֵלֶת (*tekhelet*) to the general public.

Today tallit-makers often put a stripe or two of blue across the width of the tallit, as a reminder of the Biblical mitzvah. Another reminder is the flag of the State of Israel, whose design is based on the tallit.

"the fringe at each corner" ~
From other Biblical sources we know that the edges of garments had a special significance, often symbolic of authority and power. When, for example, David cut

off the corner of King Saul's robe, Saul understood it to mean that David would surely replace him as King. The High Priest's robe is another example. It was blue (תְּכֵלֶת - *tekhelet*), and attached to its hem were pomegranates of blue, purple and scarlet.

Perhaps the Torah commanded us to put blue on the corners of every Israelite's garment to demonstrate that the people of Israel are a "Kingdom of Priests and a holy nation."

Shatnez ~

Another indication that wearing צִיצָת (*tzitzit*) is supposed to make the Israelites feel that they are dressed like kings and priests is found in the discussion about *shatnez*. In the Book of Deuteronomy, Chapter 22, just before the verse that tells us, for the second time, to *"make tassels on the four corners of the garment,"* it says that we are not permitted to make *"cloth combining wool and linen."* It seems, however, that the Torah makes an exception when it comes to priestly clothing. The special garments that the Priest wore ~ everything from his breeches to his outer robe ~ were all made of linen. They were intricately embroidered with yarn that had been spun from wool and dyed the special shade of תְּכֵלֶת (*tekhelet*).

According to traditional interpretations, the fact that the commandment to make tassels comes immediately after the commandment prohibiting shatnez means that it *is* permitted to use wool and linen together to make צִיצִת (*tzitzit*), just as it is to make the Priest's clothing.

So when you choose to put on a tallit, you not only fulfill a mitzvah, you also clothe yourself in a garment whose color (תְּכֵלֶת - *tekhelet*), whose fabric (shatnez), and whose design (צִיצִת - *tzitzit* on each corner) all have a religious and historical significance. If the archaeologists are correct that the word צִיצִת (*tzitzit*) is related to an object placed on one's garment as a sign of status, your donning a tallit is a statement of your status as part of Jewish history.

> *That shall be your fringe; look at it and recall*
> *all the commandments of Adonai and observe them.*

"look" ~
The צִיצִת (*tzitzit*) are supposed to be seen easily, especially by the person wearing them. The rabbis determined, therefore, that the tallit should only be worn during the day, and not at night. That is why the tallit is not worn at evening services, except for Kol Nidre on the eve of Yom Kippur. The Kol Nidre service is supposed to begin before dark, so the צִיצִת (*tzitzit*) can still be seen without artificial light.

"at it" ~
The Hebrew text uses the masculine singular pronoun (*oto*) after the word "look." Since the same pronoun can mean both "it" and "him," some of the Rabbis

suggest that *oto* means Him (God). The Jerusalem Talmud (Ber. 1:5, 3a) says that *oto* refers to the color blue which resembles the sea; the sea resembles the heavens; and the heavens remind us of God. In either case, looking at the צִיצָת (*tzitzit*) gives us a glimpse of God.

"and recall all of the commandments" ~
Looking at the צִיצָת (*tzitzit*) makes us think about the reason we are wearing the tallit in the first place. The צִיצָת (*tzitzit*) remind us that we are Jews; that we have a particular way of life; that we have God's mitzvot to perform. The צִיצָת (*tzitzit*) are the uniform that makes us feel part of a team with an honorable reputation.

"and observe them" ~
The English word "observe" can mean "to look at" or "to follow, obey." You may observe an accident. You should observe the law! Both of those meanings are relevant to our discussion of צִיצָת (*tzitzit*); we observe (look at) the צִיצָת (*tzitzit*), and we remember to obey (observe). There is a clear connection between seeing and doing!

In the Hebrew text, the word is וַעֲשִׂיתֶם (*v'asitem*), which also has a double meaning. At this point in the text it means "you shall do them." Earlier the same Hebrew root conveyed the meaning "make them." First we are told to make (וְעָשׂוּ - *v'asu*) the צִיצָת (*tzitzit*), and then we are told to follow (וַעֲשִׂיתֶם - *v'asitem*) the commandments. If you look closely at the verbs in the preceding paragraphs, you can see a clear progression of ideas. First comes the personal act of making the צִיצָת (*tzitzit*). Then comes the visual stimulus of seeing (observing) them. This leads to intellectual awareness of what they represent: remembering God's commandments. Finally comes the commitment to turn the awareness into the positive action of doing/observing the commandments and becoming holy.

> *So that you do not follow your heart and eyes in your lustful urge.*

"your lustful urge" ~
As we noted earlier, in most of the Jewish world a man receives a tallit from his bride and/or her family at the time of the wedding. North American Jewry is unique because it ties the wearing of a tallit to the age of bar/bat mitzvah.

The North American decision may be a very wise one. With all the changes that occur in adolescents living in an open society, they are exposed to an infinite amount of objects, ideas and situations. Some of the things that their eyes see and their hearts are attracted to may tempt them to behave inappropriately.

Indeed, the Torah places the mitzvah of צִיצָת (*tzitzit*) right after the story of the twelve spies who are sent to explore (לָתוּר - *latur*) the land of Israel while the Israelites are still wandering in the desert. Two of them came back with optimistic reports that the land was a good land, flowing with milk and honey. The other ten came back with gloomy predictions. They reported that the land was filled with enemies who could not be conquered, and they recommended that the Israelites return to Egypt. All twelve spies saw the same thing but came to opposite conclusions.

That same word ~ לָתוּר (*latur*) ~ appears in the text about צִיצָת (*tzitzit*). Don't be confused by the English translation. The same word used in the spy story to mean *explore* is used in our text to mean *do not follow* your heart and eyes in your lustful urge. Why is the same word used? In the spy story, the lesson seems to be that we use our vision to help us explore the world and gather information, but what we do with that information depends on who we are and who we want to be. The word also implies that we should look at situations carefully and not be deceived by what our eyes see (as the ten spies were deceived).

In the commandment to make צִיצָת (*tzitzit*), we are warned about things that seem attractive, but actually distance us from God. Sometimes we have to use our minds and our hearts to evaluate what are eyes are telling us. Sometimes we just have to "say no" to the temptations of our eyes.

In the commandment about the צִיצָת (*tzitzit*), we are told that the צִיצָת (*tzitzit*) are a visual reminder of all of God's commandments. What we *do* with what we see is up to us. Our eyes can lead us away from God and away from moral behavior. Our eyes can also be used to remind us who we are and who we want to be.

Observing God's commandments is a way of asserting our freedom of choice. There is no way we can hide from temptation, nor should we be denied the right to choose. Instead, we should study and follow the commandments hoping that they will help us to overcome temptation and not allow our sudden urges to control us. Religious education should teach us that sometimes we just have to say "no" to things we are tempted to do. And other times we have to perform duties that are not so pleasant, such as visiting someone seriously ill. If we only follow our eyes and heart, we may end up neglecting these important duties.

The tallit may help to keep us in line. When we look at our צִיצָת (*tzitzit*) and remember the mitzvot, our desire to do the right thing is strengthened. And at bar/bat mitzvah age we may really need ways of strengthening our desire to follow God's mitzvot.

Thus you shall be reminded to observe all My commandments and to be holy to your God. I Adonai am your God, who brought you out of the land of Egypt to be your God: I, Adonai your God.

"to be holy to your God"~
Judaism teaches that all people are created in God's image. At a wedding ceremony, one of the seven blessings recited to the bride and groom reminds them that they are created in God's image, and that they have the potential to give birth to and rear children in the image of God. So if God is holy, and we are created in the image of God, then we are holy, right? Judaism also teaches that humans have often allowed their eyes and their hearts to lead them in the wrong direction. Even in the very beginning, Adam and Eve listened to the snake instead of to God. Throughout history, humans have used their intelligence and skills to make weapons and wage wars. They have turned grapes of the vine and weeds from the earth into substances that have controlled them. They have let material wealth become a higher value than moral behavior.

What does it really mean to be holy? The Bible tells how God singled out Abraham "that he may instruct his descendants to keep the way of Adonai by doing what is just and right." In return for keeping the way of Adonai, God promised Abraham that he would make his descendants as numerous as the stars in the sky. This covenant, or agreement (the Hebrew word is

בְּרִית - *brit*) that God made with Abraham, and the Land of Israel that God promised to Abraham's descendants, demonstrated the special relationship between God and the Jewish people.

Later on, Abraham's (and Sarah's!) descendants stood at the foot of Mount Sinai, where there was a second covenant/agreement/בְּרִית (*brit*), this time between God and the entire Jewish people. They were called upon to become "a kingdom of Priests, a holy nation." They would achieve these high goals by agreeing to obey the Torah given at Sinai. When we hold up our end of the covenant, which we do by circumcising our sons and obeying the mitzvot, we demonstrate our love for God. This special relationship, the double agreement/covenant/בְּרִית (*brit*), is what makes us holy.

The content of the agreement is very important. God wants us to treat our fellow creatures in a fair and loving way. That includes everything from leaving the produce in the corners of our fields for the people who do not own property; to caring for orphans, widows, and strangers so that they, too, may live with dignity; to loaning money to the poor without charging interest. It also means being honest in our business dealings; avoiding gossip that might damage someone's reputation; speaking out to prevent injustice.

Being holy can even include things like not putting a rock in the path of blind person or not saying nasty thing to deaf people. There are so many elements of being holy; how can we remember everything we are supposed to do? The צִיצָת (*tzitzit*) we make and look upon are daily reminders of what we should be doing on our way to becoming a holy people.

"who brought you out of the land of Egypt" ~
Why does this phrase appear here, as well as in other places in the Bible and even in the Siddur (as in the Friday night קִדּוּשׁ - *kiddush*)? Does the fact that the Israelites were once slaves in Egypt have anything to do with צִיצָת (*tzitzit*)?

The Torah constantly reminds us that we were slaves in Egypt, that we were oppressed, and that we were strangers in a strange land, so that we will be especially sensitive to the rights of the poor and the strangers who live among us. Strangers in this sense are not just people we do not know; they are people who are different from us, with different backgrounds and faiths. Although they are not Israelites, strangers are also created in the image of God. We must, therefore, treat them with the same fairness and righteousness that we treat our fellow Jews. Our day-to-day efforts to achieve holiness must include protecting the rights of our non-Jewish neighbors, treating our non-Jewish employees fairly, respecting the opinions of our non-Jewish associates. The commandment of צִיצִת (*tzitzit*) reminds us of our duty to be concerned for the poor and the stranger.

Now that we have carefully analyzed the text of the mitzvah, go back and read the whole passage over again. The mitzvah of צִיצִת (*tzitzit*) should make much more sense now. But there is still more to learn about the tallit.

From Tzitzit to Tallit: What the Rabbis Taught Us

The word טַלִית (*tallit*) is never mentioned in the Bible. The Torah commands us to make צִיצִת (*tzitzit*) and to put them on the corners of our garments, but does not tell us anything more about the type of garment or how to make the צִיצִת (*tzitzit*). Tradition had to supply these answers, but where did the tradition come from?

Tradition and the Oral Law

Judaism is a religion of law, as laid out in the Torah. The Torah begins with the story of creation and ends as the Jewish people are about to enter the Promised Land. Somewhere in the middle, God revealed the Torah, known as the Written Law, at Mount Sinai. God knew that as times changed, the situations to which the law would need to be applied would change as well. So at Mount Sinai, God also gave the authority to interpret the law, and rules to guide judges when deciding how to apply the law. These interpretations were passed from generation to generation by word of mouth and became known as the Oral Law. While the Written Law was intended to be permanent, the Oral Law was seen as a continuing process of God revealing the law to the Jewish people. As new technologies developed (such as electricity and automobiles) and or the conditions of modern life changed, the Oral Law included these modifications in the understanding of the Written Law. (Eventually, centuries after the giving of the Torah, the Oral Law was written down in the *Mishnah* so that it would not be lost.)

The Hebrew word מָסַר (*masar*) means to hand over, or to pass on. The noun מָסוֹרֶת (*masoret*) means something that is passed on, or a tradition. When we refer to Jewish Law, we mean both the written and the oral law, developed by rabbis and judges throughout the ages. The garment known as the tallit and the special way in which צִיצָת (*tzitzit*) are tied are good examples of the oral law in action.

The Development of the Tallit

The word טַלִּית (*tallit*) originally meant gown or cloak, and had no special religious meaning. Only later is the term used by tradition to describe the garment requiring צִיצָת (*tzitzit*). In Biblical times, the tallit was part of a person's everyday attire and may have looked like a modern-day poncho. But styles changed and the tallit became a garment worn only for religious occasions. It was usually made of white wool with stripes woven across the width. Some tallitot had blue stripes, which served as a reminder of the original thread of תְּכֵלֶת (*tekhelet*). Today's tallitot are made of all kinds of materials and come in many different colors.

A tallit must be at least enough to cover a child just old enough to walk, but the ideal tallit is large enough to drape over an adult's shoulders and should look like a piece of clothing.

Making Tzitzit
It is the Oral Law that determined just how we should make the צִיצָת (*tzitzit*). An important part of the mitzvah of צִיצָת (*tzitzit*) is to make them with our own hands. The process is simple enough to allow people of all ages and educational backgrounds to get involved, and the sense of pride in wearing home-made צִיצָת (*tzitzit*) is one that everyone can enjoy. If you plan to make a tallit, you will need a large piece of cloth ~ cotton, wool, silk ~ big enough to drape over your shoulders, with a small hole near each corner, and four strands of wool, three the same length and the fourth somewhat longer to tie the צִיצָת (*tzitzit*).

Draw the four strands of wool through the hole. Fold the strands, making eight strings. Seven should be of equal length, and one will be quite a bit longer. Make a double knot, securing the strands to the tallit. Wind the long string, called the שָׁמָשׁ (*shamash*), around the shorter strings seven times, in the same way that

tefillin straps are wound around the arm. Make a
second double knot. Wind the long string around the
shorter strings eight times and make another double
knot. Wind the long string around the shorter strings
eleven times and make another double knot. Wind
the long string around the shorter strings thirteen
times and make a final double knot. There are now
five knots separated from each other by four sets of
between seven and thirteen "winds". Beneath the
bottom knot will hang what is left of the original eight
threads. It should be twice the knotted section's
length.

Of Strings and Knots
What is the meaning of this intricate procedure?
Tradition explains the significance of each of the
numbers. The eight strings remind us of the eighth
day of life, on which a בְּרִית (*brit*) ~ circumcision
ceremony ~ takes place. That day the child enters the
covenant with God. The five knots symbolize the
number of books of the Torah. The צִיצָת (*tzitzit*),
therefore, remind us of the covenant and the Torah.

More hidden meanings are uncovered through
Gematria, the special system that assigns a numerical
value to each letter in the Hebrew alphabet ~

אָ - *alef*=1, בּ - *bet*=2, גּ - *gimmel*=3, יּ - *yud*=10,

and so on.

Every child knows that God is One ~ אֶחָד (*ehad*) ~ (א/*alef*, ח/*het*, ד/*dalet*). אֶחָד (*ehad*) also has a numeric value of 13 (א/*alef*=1, ח/*het*=8, ד/*dalet*=4) which, obviously, is also the sum of 5 (the knots) + 8 (the strings). So the knots and the strings combined remind us of God. They also remind us of the 613 commandments. How? The word צִיצִת (*tzitzit*) has a numerical value of 600. By adding the 5 knots and the 8 strings (=13), we reach 613, the number of commandments.

We have explained the numbers of strings and knots, but why are the rows between the knots of different size? The first two sets of rows (8+7=15) have the same numeric value of the first two letters of God's name (י/*yud*=10 + ה/*heh*=5). The next set of rows (11) has the same numeric value of the last two letters of the name (ו/*vav*=6 + ה/*heh*=5). The last set of rows has 13, and we already know that the number 13 points to God, who is One.

When we look at the צִיצִת (*tzitzit*), we are reminded of the covenant, the Torah, God, and all of the commandments and are motivated to observe them. Another rabbinic tradition describes a different kind of power that the צִיצִת (*tzitzit*) hold. You remember that the last row is wound thirteen times. In rabbinic tradition, God's mercy is connected to the number 13. So God, too, wears a tallit, especially on Yom Kippur, but instead of serving as reminders of the mitzvot,

God's צִיצָת (*tzitzit*) remind God to be merciful and forgiving.

Reciting the Blessing
Rabbinic tradition requires that we recite a blessing before doing a mitzvah. The purpose of the blessing is to make us aware of God who commands us and who adds holiness to our lives. It usually (not always) contains the Torah's exact wording relating to the mitzvah, but the blessing we recite before putting on צִיצָת (*tzitzit*) does not.

Notice that instead of repeating the Torah's command to "make צִיצָת (*tzitzit*)," the blessing says that the mitzvah is the act of wrapping oneself in the צִיצָת (*tzitzit*). The Hebrew term, לְהִתְעַטֵּף (*lehitatef*), is not even found in the Torah; why is it used in the blessing?

One explanation is that the rabbinic blessing may have developed after people stopped making their own צִיצָת (*tzitzit*) and started buying them from professional צִיצָת (*tzitzit*) makers. They wore the tallit, but did not make it.

Another explanation is that the tallit was perceived as a garment that protects us not only from the elements, but from the evil forces that surround us all. Just as the Priestly *tzitz* was thought to absorb the people's sins, the צִיצָת (*tzitzit*) on the tallit were thought to absorb the evil forces and prevent them from reaching those wearing the tallit.

Women and Tzitzit

The Biblical command to make צִיצָת (*tzitzit*) seems to be directed to the entire nation of Israel. Indeed there is a Rabbinic opinion that women, like men, are obligated to fulfill this mitzvah. Another opinion states that they are not obligated, but even that source does not bar women from making and wearing צִיצָת (*tzitzit*). There is, however, a long tradition of women not fulfilling this particular mitzvah.

Summary

Clothing is worn to protect us against the elements and to cover certain parts of our body. But clothing is also a type of uniform worn to show who we are and who we want to be. The fabric and color of clothing also have symbolic value.

There is a biblical mitzvah that each person should make צִיצָת (*tzitzit*) ~ hair-like clusters ~ and put them on the edges of their garments. The corner צִיצָת (*tzitzit*) is to have a cord of blue wound around it.

In Biblical times, the place, color and fabric all symbolized that the person wearing צִיצָת (*tzitzit*) was part of a holy nation. In every age, the צִיצָת (*tzitzit*) were supposed to help us overcome the temptations which may ruin our lives.

Rabbinic tradition expanded the biblical command to make צִיצָת (*tzitzit*). They are to be attached to a garment called a tallit. The fabrics and colors of the tallit and the numerical value of the strands, knots, and twists of the צִיצָת (*tzitzit*) remind us of God, the covenant, the Torah, and the 613 commandments that help us form a holy nation. They help us overcome temptation, and even God is reminded by them on Yom Kippur. No wonder, then, that Rabbinic tradition considered enwrapping oneself in צִיצָת (*tzitzit*) to be the equivalent of all the other commandments.

The person wearing the garment should make the צִיצָת (*tzitzit*). Looking at them should cause that person to remember and observe God's laws of holiness.

The tallit is a piece of clothing with a message and with a history. We can all wrap ourselves in God's Presence, all aspire to and resist the temptations of life. This is what the tallit meant to past generations. This is what it is once again coming to mean in places like Chernovitz. This is what it can mean for whoever accepts it seriously. Make yourself צִיצָת (*tzitzit*). Wear your own tallit proudly. Understand its symbolism. Start each day sharing a moment with God. Finish each day by helping to improve the world.

Some Things to Do

If you are interested in learning more about צִיצָת (*tzitzit*) and tallit, you might want to try some of the following:

Look up the texts from the Torah about the Priestly garments and other related issues, Exodus 28 and Ezekiel 8. Talk to a marine biologist about the *Murex Trunculus*, or look up the species in an encyclopedia, to find out about this tekhelet-producing snail. Or if you are interested in how the special color is being reintroduced to use, write to the *P'til Tekhelet* Foundation.

Conduct a study of tallitot in your family. Ask your older male relatives (father, grandfather, uncle, male cousins) about their first tallitot. What were they made of? What colors did they contain? Who gave it to them? When did they first wear it? What are their most special memories associated with their tallitot? If your female relatives (mother, grandmother, aunt, female cousin) wear tallitot, ask them the same questions. Compare the answers. Share the information and stories at the next holiday gathering.

Get a Hebrew alphabet chart that includes the *Gematria* equivalents of the letters. Look up the article on *Gematria* in the *Encyclopaedia Judaica*. Practice finding the numerical value of important words such as Torah. See if you can find special meaning in the *Gematria* of your name or the names of friends.

If your congregation has its own supply of tallitot, volunteer to hand them out one Shabbat morning and to fold them neatly when services are over. Pay attention to the tallitot's similarities and differences. If the tallitot are old, you may want to look for stains, holes or loose fringes that need to be fixed. Help the *gabbai* clean and repair the tallitot.

If you do make yourself a tallit, you are going to need a tallit bag as well. This will require some sewing, so you might want to enlist the help of someone with sewing experience or a sewing machine. For now, design the kind of tallit bag you would like to have. Out of what material would you make it? What colors or symbols would you include on it? How would the bag reveal the message of what is inside? How could you make a tallit bag that would reflect elements of your Jewish identity?

May You be Wrapped in Warmth:
Creating Sacred Moments through Tallit Presentation
Susan Klingman

What better way is there to celebrate special occasions, mark rites of passage, share joys, pass on traditions, strengthen connections ~ indeed *create* sacred moments ~ than presenting, or being presented with, a tallit?

While the idea of a tallit presentation may most commonly be associated with a service in which a thirteen year old becomes a bar or bat mitzvah, this is just one of many times when tallit presentation can be used to help create personal meaning. Other possible ideas include:

- an infant receiving a tallit as part of a brit milah or naming ceremony
- an adult student receiving a tallit when he/she becomes a bar or bat mitzvah ~ or better yet when he/she *begins* a course of study

- as a closing activity after adult or family education in a synagogue or chavurah ~ especially if part of the program included creating tallitot
- as part of the celebration for engagement (the tallitot presented to the bride and groom might also serve as a chuppah on their wedding day)

The very best tallit presentation may begin with a quote, reading, or bit of information about the history or meaning of tallit in general, but also incorporates personal sentiments ~ addresses the recipient by name, includes a description or something special about the specific tallit being presented, shares family history, and communicates wishes, hopes, and prayers.

These are just a few examples of the nearly limitless possibilities for tallit presentations:

> *Hannah, a tallit may represent many things. It can be a religious symbol, a garment, a shroud, a wedding canopy, or used as an Ark to surround the Torah. It is a cloak which envelops a Jewish person, both physically and spiritually. It symbolizes a connection between our people, both those throughout history and those in our own family, throughout time and space.*
>
> *It is particularly meaningful for you to wear this tallit as you become a Bat Mitzvah. It is the same tallit I wore when I became a Bar Mitzvah, and then was worn by your sister Emily when she became a Bat Mitzvah.*

As I wrap you in this tallit, I hope that you will always remember the joys and excitement of this occasion, as well as always feel the warmth and support of your family and friends surrounding you, as it does on this day.

On behalf of mom, grandpa and grandma, and your whole family, we are so proud to witness you take your rightful place within the chain of tradition, and we now invite you to offer the blessing for wearing a tallit....

~

Jacob, as you wrap yourself in your tallit, you also wrap yourself in the folds of our tradition and experience the texture of Torah and history. As you take your place in this great community and weave your way into the tapestry of our heritage, may the many-stranded thread of your life strengthen the fabric of our people.[1]

~

Mom,

> *you have studied so long and dedicated yourself... you have made us so proud with your effort and devotion... you have earned the joy of this very special day...and it is now with that great joy that we present you with this very special tallit, decorated with the handprints of each of your children and grandchildren, so that whenever you wear it you will truly be embraced by all of us.*

~

This beautiful piece by Anita Diamant is perfect to use for an infant:

> *As we wrap you in this tallit, so may your life be*
> *wrapped in justice and righteousness.*
> *As we embrace you today, so may you embrace your*
> *tradition and your people.*
> *As your eyes are filled with wonder when you gaze at*
> *the world, so too may you be filled with wonder at the*
> *everyday miracles of life.*
> *As you startle to the world around you, so may you*
> *remain ever open both to the happiness and to the pain*
> *of those you encounter in the world.*
> *As you cry for food and comfort now, so may you one*
> *day cry out to correct the injustices of the world, to*
> *help clothe the naked and feed the hungry.*
> *As your hand tightly grasps your mother's finger,*
> *so may you grasp hold of learning and grow in*
> *knowledge and in wisdom.*

And, it may also be adapted to use for a bar/bat mitzvah:

> *Max, as you wrap yourself in your tallit:*
> *so may your life be wrapped in justice and*
> *righteousness...*
> *may you always cry out to correct the injustices*
> *of the world...*
> *may you always work to help those in need...*
> *may you always be wrapped in the love and care*
> *of your family...*
> *and, may you always be wrapped in the history*
> *and tradition of your heritage.*

~

Abraham Joshua Heschel wrote:
   "How good it is to wrap oneself in prayer, spinning
   a deep softness of gratitude to God around all
   thoughts, enveloping oneself in the silken veil of
   song."[2]

Eli, a tallit is a garment one can wear to create a
sense of personal space during prayer. By wrapping
yourself in it, or by covering your head with it, the
intention and direction of your prayers can be enhanced.
And, now as you wrap yourself in your tallit, we pray
that you too will always know how good it is to wrap
yourself in prayer. Mazal tov!

~

Josh, the Torah instructs us to make fringes on the
four corners of our garments "throughout the
generations." These fringes, called tzitzit in Hebrew,
are to help remind us of the mitzvot ~ our obligations
to God, the world, and each other. As our clothing today
is no longer a four cornered garment, we now wear a
tallit, especially for prayer.

The tallit not only serves to remind us to observe God's
commandments but it also symbolizes our connection
to the Jewish people, both throughout history and those
in our lives today.

The tallit you will wear today, as you become a Bar
Mitzvah, was worn by your father, grandfather, and
great-grandfather before you, thus truly linking you
to those who came before you. We hope that whenever
you wear it, and someday too when you pass it on,
you will feel these connections.

~

On Shabbat, that most precious of days, our ancestors dressed in their finest clothes as a sign of honor and respect. Every adult added a special garment when entering the synagogue to pray. The fringes (tzitzit) of the tallit remind us of the specialness of being Jewish, and of our readiness to fulfill mitzvot. It is a symbol that represents our our link with the past and of our connections to our people across time and space.

We present this tallit to you, Cassie, on the occasion of your becoming a Bat Mitzvah. We are very proud of you, and of your choice to purchase this tallit from Israeli merchants. We hope this both helps support our friends in Israel in some small way, as well as provides you with a symbolic connection to the land and people of Israel.

Cassie, wear your tallit proudly as you now commit yourself to our heritage and our faith.

~

The following are additional quotes and readings that may be used in creating tallit presentations such as those above. They might be read before making personal comments, used as decoration in any written material (such as a program) handed out for a service or ceremony, or adapted and/or incorporated into the presentation itself:

The tallit is a portable spiritual home in which you can wrap yourself at home, in synagogue, or when you are away on adventures and desire time for prayer, reflection or healing from a sore spot in your life.

Like paratroopers who always take their parachutes
with them when they jump from planes, those who
have begun wearing a tallit as they pray discover just
how essential it is. Like the parachute that catches the
breath of the wind, protecting those who dare to jump
into the air, the tallit ensures God's embrace for those
who dare to leap into prayer.[3]

~

Presenter:

Wrap yourself in the tallit ~ in the visions of Israel,
our people. Clothe yourself with the mantle of ethical
and spiritual responsibility. Upon your shoulders
rest the Torah and its teachings ~ you have only to
learn. Carry with you the memories of a childhood
which has passed, and be brave in facing what is yet
to come. Find the beauty of this fringed robe and bring
beauty to those you encounter on your journey.
All this, and the future too, is in your tallit.

Recipient:

I wrap myself in the tallit, in the dreams of my people.
I clothe myself with the mantle of prayer and listen to
the heartbeat of centuries.[4]

~

Weave for us a garment of brightness;
May the warp be the white light of morning,
May the weft be the red light of evening.
May the fringes be the falling rain,
May the border be the standing rainbow.
Thus weave for us a garment of brightness,
That we may walk fittingly where birds sing,
That we may walk fittingly where grass is green.[5]

~

A Life's Weave

*I like to imagine my masterpiece as a garment
continuously woven from my actions, words, intents,
and dreams. It reveals the times I have pulled the
threads too tightly, closing myself off from the world
around me, and the times I have been too lax and too
loose, threatening the fabric's integrity and mine.
My cloth has woven into it the faces and the gifts and
the hurts of the thousands of people who have touched
my life. It is honest, sometimes brutal. But mostly
as it grows day by day, it comforts and inspires me.[6]*

~

*My life has been a tapestry of rich and royal hue
An everlasting vision of the ever-changing view
A wondrous woven magic in bits of blue and gold
A tapestry to feel and see, impossible to hold.[7]*

~

*The tallit is a very personal ritual object. Usually
I wrap it around myself when joining in a prayer
community. For the tallit both creates a private
space for me and links me with Jewish tradition.
It emphasizes my connection to my people while
also offering me spiritual privacy. I am alone and
in community at the same time.[8]*

~

*Recalling the generations, I wrap myself in the tallit.
May my mind be clear, my spirit open, as I envelop
myself in prayer. Here I envelop myself in a fringed
garment in order to recall and to preserve the tradition
of the generations in order to direct my heart.[9]*

~

From where was the light created? The Holy One of Blessing wrapped Himself in a white tallit and the light of Her radiance shone from one end of the world to the other. Holy One of Blessing Your Presence fills creation. You make us holy with Your commandments and bid us to wrap ourselves in the fringed garment.[10]

~

As I wrap myself in the tallit, I fulfill the mitzvah of my Creator, as written in the Torah:
    "They shall make fringes for themselves on the corners of their garments throughout the generations."

Even as I cover myself with this tallit, so may my soul be robed in the garment of God's light.
    Bless Adonai, O my soul!
    Adonai my God, how great You are;
    You are robed in glory and majesty.
    You wrap yourself in light as in a garment;
    You stretch out the heavens like a curtain.[11]

~

Holy One of Blessing, Your presence fills creation. You make us holy with Your commandments and bid us to wrap ourselves in the fringed garment.[12]

~

And for everyone who presents, receives, or dons a tallit:

Let yourself feel what it means to enter this fabric sukkah ~ a shelter of peace.[13]

---

[1] Adapted from a quote by Jonathan Kremer.

---

[2] Rabbi Abraham Joshua Heschel in *Man's Quest for God*.

[3] Adapted from writings by the CLAL Faculty. [CLAL is the National Jewish Center for Learning and Leadership.]

[4] Author unknown ~ may also be used separately.

[5] *Song of the Loom*, Twea Indian.

[6] Author unknown.

[7] *Tapestry*, Carole King.

[8] Attributed to "L.B."

[9] Marcia Falk, *The Book of Blessings*.

[10] From the prayer book *V'taheir Libeinu* (Congregation Beth-El, Sudbury, MA.)

[11] From the prayer book *Mishkan Tefilah: The Siddur for Reform Jewish Prayer*.

[12] Contemporary adaptation of the traditional blessing for donning a tallit.

[13] Author unknown.

Acknowledgements

The Tallit and Its Messages by Dov Peretz Elkins, from *The Tallit*.
Reprinted by permission.

A Message from Outer Space by Jack Riemer.
Reprinted by permission.

Knots: a Sermon for Shelah by Rabbi Shamai Kanter.
Reprinted by permission.

"And the tzitzit shall be for you ~ A Bar Mitzvah D'var Torah"
by Alon Futterman. Reprinted by permission.

Curbing Your Lustful Eyes by Pinhas H. Peli, Jerusalem Post,
June 28, 1986. Reprinted by permission of *The Jerusalem Post*.

The Fringed Garment: The Mitzvah of Tzitzit by
Rabbi Hershel Matt. Reprinted by permission of Gustine Matt.

My Grandfather's Tallis by Rabbi Steven Carr Reuben.
Reprinted by permission.

The Tallit on Kol Nidre by Rabbi Steve Schwartz.
Reprinted by permission.

*From Our Own Clothing to God's Own Throne: The True Meaning
of the Tallit* by Peretz Rodman. Reprinted by permission.

Lehitatef Batzitzit: Recovering the Meaning of the Tallit by
Kenneth R. Leitner. *The Reconstructionist*, January/February
1988, pp. 13-16. Reprinted by permission.

The Tallit and its Symbolism by Martin Samuel Cohen. *Conservative
Judaism*, Vol. 44 #3, Spring 1992, pp. 3-15. Reprinted by
permission of the author and of *Conservative Judaism*.

Tekhelet ~ A Royal Reminder by Mordecai Kaplan. Proceedings of
RA Convention 1969, p. 35. Reprinted by permission.

Another Tallit by S.Y. Agnon. Translated by Jules Harlow.
Commentary, Vol. 30 #4, October 1960.
Reprinted by permission.

A Stranger's Tallit by Allan Rabinowitz. Reprinted by permission.

My Father's Tallit and the Sefer Torah by Ruthy Bodner.
Reprinted by permission.

The Babies' Aliyah in Jerusalem by Judith Weisberg. *Moment*,
October, 1998, p. 37. Reprinted by permission.

Contributors

Rabbi Dov Peretz Elkins is author and editor of over 30 books in Judaism, spirituality and human relations.

Steven Schwarzman is a second-career rabbinical student at the Jewish Theological Seminary, having worked as a translator, editor, and writer in Israel and the United States.

S.Y. Agnon was the first Israeli to win a Nobel Prize.

Yehuda Amichai was a world renowned Israeli poet.

Anat Bental was a young poet from Haifa who was tragically killed in a car accident when she was in her early twenties in 1975.

Ruthy Bodner lives in New Jersey with her husband and two children.

Ruth F. Brin is best known for her liturgical poetry, which is found in the prayerbooks of the Conservative, Reform and Reconstructionist movements; she has also published personal poetry, children's books, and articles in periodicals.

Rabbi Nina Beth Cardin is the Director of the Department of Jewish Life of the JCCs of Greater Baltimore. Her most recent book is *The Tapestry of Jewish Time: A Spiritual Guide to Holidays and Life-cycle Events* (Behrman House).

Martin Samuel Cohen is the Rabbi of Shelter Rock Jeewish Center, Roslyn, NY.

Alon Futterman is the son of Rabbi Matt and Chanah Futterman, of Ashkelon, Israel.

Rabbi Jules Harlow, Founding Editor of The Rabbinical
Assembly, is a liturgist and translator.

Reuven Hammer is past president of the Rabbinical Assembly
and author of several books including *Or Hadash, A commentary
on Siddur Sim Shalom.*

Shamai Kanter is a retired Conservative rabbi.

Mordecai Kaplan was Dean of the Teachers Institute of the
Jewish Theological Seminary, where he was also Professor of
Philosophy of Religions, and later founded the Reconstructionist
Momement.

Abraham Kinstlinger is an attorney living in Englewood, New
Jersey. His father survived the Holocaust by escaping from
Plaszow concentration camp and fighting with a partisan group
in Poland until the end of the war.

Susan Klingman creates and designs custom worship and
education materials for synagogues, religious schools, and
Jewish life-cycle events.

Susan Mitrani Knapp is a second-career rabbinical student at
the Jewish Theological Seminary. She believes she serves God
and the Jewish people best when she combines her open heart
with the sacred texts of the tradition.

Rabbi Mordecai Kornfeld of Jerusalem is founder of the
Dafyomi Advancement Forum.

Kenneth R. Leitner serves as rabbi of Congregation Kneses
Tiferet Israel, Port Chester, NY

Rabbi Hershel Matt was a beloved spiritual leader, passionate about serving God through the power of prayer and the enhancement of ritual, and passionate about serving the Jewish people.

Karen Misler lives in Teaneck, New Jersey with her husband Barry Feigenbaum and two children, Jeremy and Stephanie. She is on the Executive Board of Congregation Beth Sholom, a traditional egalitarian Conservative synagogue in Teaneck. Karen works as a freelance editor and market research consultant.

Rabbi Pinhas H. Peli was Blechner Professor of Jewish Thought and Literature, Ben-Gurion University of the Negev.

Rabbi Dr. Menachem Raab has held positions in the rabbinate and in education. For a number of years he served as Dean of the Hillel Community Day School and High School, North Miami Beach, Florida. He has contributed articles to numerous publications including Hadarom, Jewish Education, Dor le Dor, and others. He currently resides in Israel.

Allan Rabinowitz grew up in New Jersey and worked as a journalist in California, Colorado and Wisconsin before becoming a licensed tour guide in Israel. He has taught and lectured widely on Israel, published short stories and essays, for six years wrote a travel column for the Jerusalem Post, and recently completed a novel. He lives in Jerusalem with his family.

Steven Carr Reuben is the Rabbi of Kehillat Israel in Pacific Palisades, California.

Rabbi Jack Riemer is the co-editor of *Ethical Wills*, the editor of *Jewish Reflections on Death*, and editor of *New Prayers for the High Holy Days*.

Peretz Rodman is a Jerusalem-based rabbi, teacher, writer, and translator. The tallit presented to him at his ordination by the Schechter Institute of Jewish Studies has a strand of t'khelet in the tzitzit at each corner. For information on obtaining tzitzit with p'til t'khelet, see www.tekhelet.org.

Rabbi Steve Schwartz is spiritual leader at Beth El Congregation, Baltimore.

Rabbi Moshe Tutnauer lives in Jerusalem.

Dvora E. Weisberg is assistant professor of rabbinics at the Hebrew Union College-Jewish Institute of Religion in Los Angeles.

Judith Weisberg is a writer living in Jerusalem.

Rabbi Ari Z. Zivotofsky, Ph.D. is on the faculty of the Gonda Brain Science Center, Bar Ilan University, Israel.

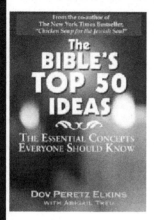

Made in the USA
Las Vegas, NV
24 July 2022

52089984R00167